WIN THE HEART

Other Titles by Mark Miller

The High Performance Series

Chess Not Checkers
Leaders Made Here
Talent Magnet

Other Books

The Heart of Leadership
The Secret of Teams

Coauthored with Ken Blanchard

Great Leaders Grow
The Secret

Field Guides

The Heart of Leadership Field Guide
The Secret of Teams Field Guide

Field Guides Coauthored with Randy Gravitt

The Secret Field Guide
Leaders Made Here Field Guide
Chess Not Checkers Field Guide
Talent Magnet Field Guide
Win the Heart Field Guide

WIN THE HEART

HOW TO CREATE A CULTURE OF FULL ENGAGEMENT

MARK MILLER

BK®

Berrett–Koehler Publishers, Inc.

Berrett-Koehler Publishers, Inc.
1333 Broadway, Suite 1000
Oakland, CA 94612-1921
Tel: (510) 817-2277
Fax: (510) 817-2278
www.bkconnection.com

ORDERING INFORMATION
Quantity sales. Special discounts are available on quantity purchases by corporations, associations, and others. For details, contact the "Special Sales Department" at the Berrett-Koehler address above.
Individual sales. Berrett-Koehler publications are available through most bookstores. They can also be ordered directly from Berrett-Koehler: Tel: (800) 929-2929; Fax: (802) 864-7626; www.bkconnection.com.
Orders for college textbook / course adoption use. Please contact Berrett-Koehler: Tel: (800) 929-2929; Fax: (802) 864-7626.

Distributed to the U.S. trade and internationally by Penguin Random House Publisher Services.

Printed in the United States

Berrett-Koehler books are printed on long-lasting acid-free paper. When it is available, we choose paper that has been manufactured by environmentally responsible processes. These may include using trees grown in sustainable forests, incorporating recycled paper, minimizing chlorine in bleaching, or recycling the energy produced at the paper mill.

Library of Congress Cataloging-in-Publication Data
Names: Miller, Mark, 1959- author.
Title: Win the heart : how to create a culture of full engagement / Mark Miller.
Description: First edition. | Oakland, CA : Berrett-Koehler Publishers, [2019]
Identifiers: LCCN 2018041236 | ISBN 9781523099870 (print hardcover)
Subjects: LCSH: Leadership.
Classification: LCC HD57.7 .M538 2019 | DDC 658.3/12--dc23
LC record available at https://lccn.loc.gov/2018041236

First Edition
26 25 24 23 22 21 20 19 10 9 8 7 6 5 4 3 2 1

Text designer: Marin Bookworks
Cover designer: Lindsay Miller
Horseshoe Heart: HammeredForge.com
Editing: PeopleSpeak

Contents

Introduction

The life of a leader can be hectic. On most days, we have a dizzying array of problems screaming for our attention—internal pressures such as staffing, quality, and capacity issues combined with external storm clouds propelling the war for talent, competitive pressures, and ever-changing governmental regulations, to name just a few.

In the midst of this cacophony is brewing a threat to our organizations, often unseen and unheard above the daily din—the thief of sales, profits, customer satisfaction, and the pride in a job well done: low employee engagement.

The data on this topic is so consistently shocking, most leaders have become numb to the annual statistics. Some have even retreated into denial and chosen to stop thinking and talking about engagement. This is not the answer.

Engagement matters for several reasons.

First, there are the people. Their work life matters. As leaders, we have an opportunity to help people find meaning and purpose in their work. We can create a place where they can bring their best selves to work every day. The workplace we create determines, to a large extent, how engaged someone is at work. Do your people go home *energized* or *disempowered* at the end of a long day? We really do have the responsibility to decide.

Leaders should also care deeply about engagement because of the opportunity it presents. If we can harness the untapped potential buried deep within the hearts of our people, we can turn engagement from a liability into a real, sustainable competitive advantage and usher in gains in productivity unseen since the industrial revolution!

Finally, for many organizations, engagement is the final hurdle to becoming a high performance organization. I outlined this journey in my book *Chess Not Checkers* and have done a deep dive on some of the best practices in other recent books. For those who are not familiar with the concepts, here is a ten-second summary:

All high performance organizations have four things in common. They **Bet on Leadership** (*Leaders Made Here*), **Act as One** (*Talent Magnet*), and **Win the Heart** (covered in this book). These three "moves" enable them to **Excel at Execution** (to be covered in a book to be released in the spring of 2020).

Here's my encouragement to you: keep an open mind, check your assumptions about engagement at the door, and get ready to unleash the full potential of your people and your organization.

Epiphany

Life was good: the kids were thriving, Megan was happy and involved in the community, and their income was better than it had ever been. And yet, at work, something wasn't right—and Blake was having trouble putting his finger on it.

He had read the reports, studied the financials, talked to customers, and listened intently to what his employees were saying about the state of the business. Blake was not merely listening to the music; he was attempting to hear the space between the notes, attempting to discern what was true but unspoken.

The best leaders all have the ability to see the unseen: changing trends, strategies that are coming to the end of their productive life, the untapped potential in people, and even threats just beyond the horizon. This leadership intuition compelled Blake to seek answers.

As he drove to work one morning, he considered the facts as he saw them: The organization's performance had plateaued. The competition was slowly gaining ground, but no one had even seemed to notice. People showed up, did their work, and went home.

He believed his people were just going through the motions. Now, their discontent was almost palpable; he sensed it in the shadows, avoiding for now the bright light of the monthly financials. Blake could imagine everyone in the organization calling out in silent desperation, *I really don't care!*

That's it! he thought. That was the problem.

Blake didn't know what to do with this epiphany. However, once a problem was identified, even the faint outline of one, he wanted to move toward a solution—and fast.

As he made his way into the parking lot, the root cause of this dilemma was already beginning to crystalize in his mind.

A combination of busyness, uncertain markets, surging competition, and turnover on his own leadership team had caused Blake to lose sight of his people. In an instant, it was clear.

Their current reality and the malaise that had now overcome his organization was a direct consequence of his choices as a leader.

Before Blake made his way to his office, he stopped by to see Charles, the head of their people function.

"Good morning, Blake," Charles said. "How was your weekend?"

"Okay," Blake began, clearly distracted by his newfound insight. "The kids are good, Megan is good. Everything is good . . . and that's the problem."

"Whoa! Where did that come from?"

"I've been thinking," Blake said.

"And . . ." Charles waited.

"Things are just okay . . . and I think that's a problem. We need to create a plan."

Their current reality and the malaise that had now overcome his organization was a direct consequence of his choices as a leader.

"Slow down. I lost you at 'that's a problem,'" Charles smiled.

"I know. It sounds loony. You and I, and the entire team, have worked really hard over the last few years."

"We have," Charles nodded.

"And we've seen some improvements," Blake continued. "But I'm not convinced . . ." His voice trailed off.

"Convinced of what?" Charles asked.

"Let me ask you a question," Blake said.

"Okay, shoot."

"Are you happy at work? Are you fully engaged? Do you really care?"

"What?" Charles asked. "Say all that again."

"Are you really happy at work?"

"What does that have to do with anything?" Charles asked.

"Everything!" Blake said.

"You're going to have to say more."

"Are you happy, fulfilled, excited, motivated, and energized to be at work today?"

Charles had known Blake for many years, but he was the CEO and his boss, so he paused before responding. "Well . . ." He paused again and then spoke slowly. "Blake, you are setting the bar really, really high. I am thankful to have a job, I appreciate all you and the company have done for me personally, but I'm not sure what you are suggesting is realistic. It is *just* a job."

"That's it!" Blake exclaimed. "You just articulated what I've been feeling. I think that's our problem."

"I didn't know we had a problem," Charles said.

"It's a huge problem! If leaders feel this way, what about the people building our products and serving our customers—how do they feel? Do they see their work as 'just a job' too?"

"I suppose so."

"Think about the implications. If people see their work as *just a job*, why would they bring their full, best self to work? Why would they go the extra mile?

Why would they take risks? Why would they challenge the status quo? Why would they help their coworkers? Why would they suggest improvements? Why would they care?"

Blake continued, "I think this explains a lot."

"Like what?" Charles asked.

"Sluggish performance, low urgency and energy, indifference toward customers and the competition. It may also explain why this place is a ghost town at 5:01 every day. Have you noticed people like to back into the parking spaces?"

"Yes—I always wondered why they do that."

"Maybe so they can make a quick escape."

Both men chuckled, but it was forced because they knew Blake's joke might have some truth to it.

"So, what do we do with this hypothesis?" Blake asked.

If people see their work as *just a job*, why would they bring their full, best self to work?

"About the parking?"

"No! I don't think people really care about their work, coworkers, or the organization."

"Whoa—you've just blown this thing way out of proportion," Charles said. "We have very good people."

"If I am correct, this is *not* a reflection on the people. This is my fault, and yours too, and every other leader in the organization. We are to blame."

"I'm not sure I totally get that 'leap of blame,' but we can talk more about that. Why don't we de-escalate this and see if we can collect some data?"

"What do you have in mind?"

"What we're discussing is called engagement. There are assessments we can use to find the truth. And *if* there is a problem, we can fix it.

"Then let's do that as soon as possible," Blake said.

Engagement

Charles and his team immediately began selecting the assessment instrument they would use to take the pulse of the workforce. If he was honest with himself, he knew he should have done this sooner. As a seasoned HR leader, he knew engagement had been all the rage for more than a decade. However, his default had been to focus on what he believed to be most important—selection, compensation, and benefits. Admittedly, the softer factors impacting the emotional commitment of employees he had largely left to chance.

"Good morning!" Charles said to his leadership team, who were assembled for their regularly scheduled meeting. Peggy, Kim, Gary, Rose, and Ben had all been with him from the beginning of his short tenure.

"Here's the situation," Charles began. "Blake and I have been talking, and we believe we need to assess our employee engagement. Have any of you ever used an engagement survey in your previous companies?"

Everyone's hand went up except Peggy's; she was the youngest member of the team and had joined the organization just out of college.

"That's good! You'll have the chance to coach me; I've never used a formal survey. Which instruments have you used in the past?" Charles went to the board and began to field the responses from the team. A moment later, he stepped back and looked at the list. "This is incredible; there are four of you, and you've used thirteen different assessments!"

Shaking his head in disbelief, Charles continued, "I guess we should talk about what you liked and didn't like . . . and how the assessment helped you drive improvement."

Gary was the first to speak. "Look, I can see why this is important work—goodness, engagement has been a big deal for years—maybe forever. However, I think our first issue is to define it. What exactly are we trying to measure or assess?"

"I think that's one reason there are so many different surveys out there. Very few agree on what engagement is to begin with," Kim added.

"Okay, let's get started," Charles said. "Everyone write your definition of engagement on a 3 x 5 card. Who knows? Maybe we will be closer than we think."

After everyone finished the assignment, Charles went back to the board and began to write:

Engagement is . . .

- *The emotional commitment a person has for his/her work*
- *The invisible force driving discretionary effort*
- *A reflection of the heart*
- *A measure of effort in the face of difficulty*
- *How hard someone will work when things get hard*
- *A psychological condition affecting energy, effort, and enthusiasm*
- *How much a person is invested in his/her work*

"Okay, wait, there are six of us and seven definitions," Kim pointed out.

"Yeah, I know," Ben confessed. "I cheated. I wrote two."

"You always were an overachiever," Rose said. "We'll forgive you—one more time."

"I can see truth in all of these statements—it also underscores our challenge. I agree with Gary's question. What are we really trying to measure?" Kim asked. "If we can answer that one, I suppose we can find a way to measure it."

"Good call," Charles said. "Since there is not a universally accepted definition, why don't we create our own? How do *we* want to define engagement?"

After a long debate, Kim said, "Here's what I think I've heard. Collectively, we believe engagement is a measure of how much someone cares. Is that correct?"

"I'm not sure," Peggy said.

"Maybe . . . ," Ben added.

"What's your hesitation?" Rose probed.

"Does it say enough?" Ben asked.

"What else would you want?" Gary chimed in.

"Care about what?" Peggy asked. "It feels too open-ended. Should we reference the work, coworkers, the organization . . . maybe?" she suggested in a half-hearted question.

"It could be how much they care about their hobby, school, church, or even their family. That's why we don't need to specify—engagement can serve as the measure of care in any environment," Kim added.

"Agreed, engagement is a life issue, but for our purposes, I like what Peggy suggested," Charles said. "We need to focus on care at work."

"My issue is different," Gary added. "Care is just too soft. I want people to work harder and smarter. Where is the fruit? Where is the effort? Where are the results?"

"If you care more, do you think you will work harder and do more?" Peggy asked.

"Probably," Gary said.

"It makes sense to me; the more you care, the more effort you bring to any given situation," Kim said.

"Looking back at the board," Ben said, "I think you are all right—engagement is a condition of the heart reflecting an individual's level of genuine care for their work, coworkers, and the organization. And if the level of care is high enough, it will result in energy, effort, enthusiasm, and initiative. However, my vote is to keep it simple."

"Okay," Charles said, "What do you propose?"

Ben looked around the table, stood up, went to the board and wrote:

Engagement = Level of Care

"I like it," Kim said.

"It is really clean," Rose said, nodding, "and profound in its simplicity. If someone really cares, we'll see it in their attitude and actions. We can agree this would equate to high engagement. The flip side is also true. If someone doesn't really care . . . well, we've all seen the consequences of that scenario."

"I like it too . . . ," Gary said, stopping short.

Peggy picked up on his hesitation and asked, "Why do you like it, Gary?"

"Because I understand it," he said. Everyone laughed.

"That's a good sign for all of us," Charles added. "If people don't get it, you can forget it."

"Here's what I like," Peggy said. "If we could measure *and* affect a person's level of care, I believe we could fundamentally change this place . . . for the better!"

"Let's begin by looking for a way to measure how much people around here really care," Rose suggested.

"I'll take that assignment and report back next week," Kim said.

Reality

Kim found an assessment that was close to what they wanted, but it attempted to measure much more than the level of care. However, the team decided they could extrapolate what they needed. Charles shared the team's plan with the executive committee and asked Blake to send an email to the entire organization with a link to the survey.

In Charles's monthly meeting with Blake, the "issue," as Blake called it, was the only item on the agenda.

"How's it going with the survey?" Blake asked.

"The response rate has been low so far."

"How low?"

"Ten percent."

"Really?" Blake responded in an aggravated tone. "This is a problem! And it's just another symptom of the bigger issue. People don't even care enough to fill out the survey!"

"Hold on," Charles protested. "Don't jump to any conclusions about the overall level of care. Our people are busy."

"I can't believe our people couldn't find ten minutes over a two-week period to do this. Let's call an all-staff meeting."

"Everyone? Are you sure? You know we don't do that very often. It might scare people."

"I'm scared of the consequences if we don't meet."

~

When the staff gathered Friday morning, rumors were flying. One by-product of low engagement is often low trust. Blake knew this and wanted to address it head-on.

"Good morning!" Blake said in his typical warm and energetic tone. "It is fantastic to see everyone in the same room. First, an overdue thank-you from me for your efforts to maintain our market share in the face of increased competition. As many of you know, we are working to create new products and services to help us be even more competitive. However, today is not about products and services; we are not announcing a merger, a reorganization, a downsizing, or any other structural changes. I called this meeting to discuss something even more important—you.

"We've been heads down for a long time—focused on today's work and today's challenges. From time to time, this may be necessary. However, leadership must always make time to do the heads-up work of the organization. We have to rise above the daily distractions; we must be sure we invest enough time today to ensure we will have a better tomorrow. I have not always done this well.

We have to rise above the daily distractions; we must be sure we invest enough time today to ensure we will have a better tomorrow.

"One area I have not given enough focus is our culture. For this I apologize. The tyranny of the urgent is an ever-present challenge, but I am recommitting to you to strengthen our culture—to build on the best parts of what we've created here and eradicate the behaviors that undermine our long-term success.

"A huge part of our future is you. I want to create a workplace in which you can thrive. Honestly, my hunch is we have much to do in this arena, but to move forward with purpose, we need more specific information on what needs to be improved. That's why I sent you the link to a survey a few weeks ago.

"Here's what I am asking each of you to do today as soon as we leave this room. Please go and complete the assessment. There are four things you need to know:

"One, your responses will be anonymous—the survey is being tabulated by a trusted third party.

"Two, we will share the findings with you—all of them . . . the good, bad, and ugly. Three, we will also share our response to the issues. And finally, I will personally read every comment.

"My commitment to you is to make this an amazing place to work—every job, every department, every shift. To make good on this promise, we need to hear from you. Thanks for partnering with us on the journey. Please complete your survey today."

As Blake left the podium, Charles said, "That was outstanding."

"We'll see," Blake said. "It was only outstanding if they complete the survey."

~

On the following Wednesday, Charles was ready to share the results of the survey.

"Good morning, Blake!"

"Do you have the report?" Blake asked.

"I do. I have good news and bad news. Let me begin with the good news," Charles said. "I underestimated the power of your talk. I need to upgrade my assessment from outstanding to phenomenal!

We have received a completed assessment from 81 percent of the staff."

"Okay, now for the bad news . . . ," Blake said as he braced himself.

"Engagement is awful. Tragically low, according to our vendor. Your instincts were right on target; we do have a problem."

"Somehow that doesn't make me feel any better."

"Yes, I know. I'm just glad we have the data." For the next few minutes, Charles reviewed the numbers with Blake. He explained the rating scale: a rating of 1 indicated someone strongly disagreed with a statement; a rating of 3 represented neither agreement nor disagreement; and if someone rated a statement with a 5, it indicated strong agreement. Of all the responses, these troubled Blake the most:

- I believe in the vision of the organization = 2.4
- I feel valued for the work I do = 2.0
- I am given opportunities to make decisions that matter = 1.9
- I believe it is safe to voice dissenting opinions with my supervisor = 1.7

"How did we get here?" Blake said, staring blankly across the room.

"Not sure exactly," Charles said, "but we'll make it better."

Blake grimaced and asked, "What's next?"

"My team is going to dig into the details and begin creating some plans regarding how we change our current reality." Charles continued, "We have to start where we are, but we certainly don't have to stay here."

"Thanks. I know. I just hate having dropped the ball like this," Blake confided.

"Me too." Looking for something else to say, Charles added, "What are your next steps?"

"I am going to begin reading the comments; it looks like we received a lot."

"We did."

"And then, I'm going to talk to Debbie."

"Who's Debbie?"

"My first mentor. I haven't seen her in a while, and I think it's time for a visit."

Reunion

Debbie Brewster, more than anyone else beyond Blake's dad, the venerable Jeff Brown, had shaped him as a leader. She taught him that his capacity to grow would determine his capacity to lead while setting him on the path to develop his leadership character. Her challenge changed the trajectory of his life: "If your heart is not right, no one cares about your skills."

Most recently, Debbie had introduced Blake to Jack Deluca. Jack, the former world-renowned CEO, taught Blake the "moves" required to create a high performance organization. Blake remembered Jack's insistence on the folly of trying to execute at a world-class level if your people were not fully engaged. As Jack would say, "Without engaged people, excellence will be sporadic at best—sustained greatness always just beyond your grasp."

Blake was a little bit anxious about visiting Debbie. He was not good at staying in touch, and Debbie had a penchant for international travel. Each of their habits played a part in allowing them to drift apart. Her move to the West Coast and the miles now between them had created yet another impediment to their ongoing relationship. All this notwithstanding, Blake wanted to reconnect.

When he called, she offered her typical response: "Absolutely!" She had always made herself available to Blake and many other younger leaders. Blake was headed to Napa Valley!

Once in Napa, Blake easily found his way to Debbie's place. He nervously approached the front door, rang the bell, and waited. When Debbie opened the door, time stood still. In an instant, Blake was transported in his mind back to the coffee shop where she had consoled, coached, and challenged him over the years.

"Hello," she said. "Wonderful to see you!" She gave Blake a big hug.

"Agreed," Blake said.

"Please come in!"

"Your home is lovely. How long have you lived here?"

"Well, after John died, I asked myself of all the places he and I had visited over the years, what was my favorite? Napa won that contest hands down. So, after some extended travel, I came here and built this place—I guess that would have been almost ten years ago."

"I remember the last time we talked, when you introduced me to Jack, you were under construction then."

"You're right . . . hated to hear about Jack's death—a terrible loss," Debbie said. "I'm sure the time you two spent together was valuable."

"Absolutely!" Blake said. "He taught me so much. He even gave me the primer on how to address my current challenges, but I obviously need a refresher."

"Or, maybe an advanced course," Debbie smiled.

"I'll take all the help I can get," Blake said. "But before we jump in to my issues, I need to say something . . . I assume I'm the worst mentee you've ever had. I have not stayed in touch, and I apologize for that. But I need to tell you, the lessons you taught me are with me every day. Other than my dad, you have done more to shape my leadership than anyone else. Thank you!"

"You are so kind. No apology needed. The time we spent together was what the season demanded. Now, here we are again, and I want to help, but first, give me an update on Megan, Clint, and Kristen."

The way Debbie set Blake at ease was uncanny; her ability to make others comfortable was one of her most outstanding traits. This was not the first time Debbie had made Blake feel important. He wondered if he could ever learn to help others feel the same way.

The time flew by; it was a reunion of sorts—lots of updates, laughs, and photos. Blake's pictures were mostly of his kids, and Debbie had some stunning photos from her travels.

"You've become an outstanding photographer," Blake said.

"Thanks. A lot of practice," she smiled, "and Photoshop.

"Tell me about these challenges you referenced. They must be significant if you were willing to fly across the country to meet with me," Debbie suggested.

"Well . . . I think I know the problem—I guess I should say, problems plural, because I assume the root cause is not as obvious as it may appear."

"How does it appear?"

"It looks like the people at my company are totally disengaged."

"How do you know that?"

"Two sources of data—qualitative and quantitative. First the qualitative . . ." Blake proceeded to explain his feeling about the state of his workforce. "Now for the data." He gave Debbie a copy of the summary report.

"I see," Debbie said as she scanned the document. "Okay, got it. What are you going to do next?"

"I'm not sure," Blake confessed. "You *are* my next step."

"Based on what I see here, you are right to be concerned, but heartfelt concern and even noble intentions are no substitute for actions. You and your leaders must win the heart of your entire workforce—one person at a time."

"Win the heart; that's the same language Jack used to describe this issue," Blake recalled.

"He was a smart man. Your father knew this was important as well. That's why he taught me and others a fundamental part of our role as leaders is to engage and develop others."

"Can you tell me more?" Blake asked.

"Engaging others is at the core of a leader's responsibilities. A leader who cannot effectively engage others will always struggle—destined to live outside the circle of real victory. All he or she accomplishes will pale in comparison to what might have been if the leader had been successful at winning the hearts of the people.

"We must always remember it is up to our people to fulfill the grand promises we make; they decide how much they really care about the work and the organization. Our people decide whether the vision will become a reality or remain a fragile figment of a leader's imagination. These decisions are theirs and theirs alone . . . but the inputs to these decisions are ours. The things leaders do, or fail to do, create, lift, or diminish engagement.

"It's really straightforward: You created the current level of engagement in your organization. If it's not where it should be, you can fix it." Debbie paused. "I think you've got what you need to move forward."

"Ho, ho . . . hold on!" Blake stuttered. "It sounds like you're about to wish me luck and send me on my way. I need answers—more than answers, I need action items."

"I get it; I really do," Debbie said. "This is hard. For some leaders, engaging others is the hardest part of leadership."

"Why is that?" Blake asked.

"I'm not sure. My theory is some leaders find it easier to think about other things—vision, alignment, execution, and the daily grind. People issues are unique, often complicated, and sometimes messy. People have individual needs, and as a leader, you quickly realize one-size solutions will not work. All of this makes engagement a real challenge.

"However, just because it's difficult doesn't mean you can take a pass—as you know by now, this issue is absolutely critical. If you don't address low levels of engagement, you will destine your organization to mediocrity, irrelevance, or worse. I applaud your efforts to work on this. It's a sign of your growing maturity as a leader."

"I agree with the difficult part," Blake said shaking his head.

"You know, you're in good company."

"What do you mean?"

"Your dad struggled with this, too."

"Really? I never knew that."

"Absolutely. Yet he was still a great leader," Debbie affirmed.

"Help me reconcile those two thoughts: great leader who struggled with the topic of engagement?"

"The fact that your father acknowledged the importance of engagement and understood his own strengths and opportunities as a leader led him into a productive struggle with the issue . . . his ongoing efforts enabled him to be an extremely effective and beloved leader.

If you don't address low levels of engagement, you will destine your organization to mediocrity, irrelevance, or worse.

"Your dad was determined to lead well. He would not fall into the trap of denial and distraction. Lesser leaders often diminish and dismiss this issue; they attempt to lead with little concern for the engagement of their team. These leaders never know how much influence they could have had.

"Jeff worked on this as long as I knew him and was committed to helping other leaders do the same." Debbie turned, looking at the sunset. "I wish he had finished the book," she said softly.

"Book? What book?" Blake asked.

"You didn't know? Your dad spent years studying the topic of engagement. His plan was to write a book about what he was learning."

"Why didn't I know about this?" Blake said.

"I guess because he never finished it. Why don't you ask your mom about it? Surely, she knew. Who knows, maybe there's a manuscript in her basement?" She smiled.

"This is big!" Blake said.

Sensing the meeting was coming to an end, Blake wanted to say a proper good-bye. He had always regretted not having one more opportunity to thank Jack for their time together; he didn't want to make the same mistake with Debbie.

"Thanks for this time today. You are such a gift to me. But more important than today, thanks for all you've invested in me over the years. There's not been a day over the last fifteen years you haven't influenced my life and leadership. You have made me a better husband, father, and leader. Thanks for believing in me when I didn't believe in myself."

"It's been my pleasure. Let's agree today, we won't wait so long to meet again. Please tell Megan and your mom I said hello!"

The Box

As excited as Blake had been to see Debbie, he was now even more excited to see his mom. He called her on the way back to the airport.

"Hi, Mom! How are you?"

"Everything is wonderful here. How about you?"

"Good. I'm in Napa Valley."

"Napa? Why are you in Napa?"

"I just met with Debbie Brewster."

"How is she?"

"Healthy, happy, and helpful, as usual. She said to tell you hello. I have a question. Debbie told me about a book Dad was working on when he died."

"Yes, what about it?"

"You never mentioned it," Blake said.

His mom offered no response.

"Do you know if Dad had any notes or maybe a manuscript at the house?"

"I'm sure his notes are here, somewhere . . ." she offered hesitantly.

"Do you have plans tomorrow morning? I know you like to play tennis on Saturdays."

"No, we're off this weekend."

"I'll come by the house tomorrow morning if that's okay."

"Come early and you can have some pancakes," she said. Blake could hear the smile in her voice.

~

The next morning, Blake was up earlier than usual. He drove the hour across town to his mom's house, arriving just in time for breakfast.

"This is a pleasant surprise—I really didn't expect to see you this early."

"The pancakes, Mom—you knew I wouldn't miss them," Blake said, sounding like a hungry teenager.

As the two sat and chatted, Blake quickly turned the conversation to the book.

"This book must be important to you."

"Debbie said Dad researched it for years."

"Yes, he did. We even visited a few places during our family vacations so your dad could talk to people about how to better serve his people."

"Now, that helps bring a few things into perspective. I always wondered about some of our stops during family road trips. Where are his files?"

"In the attic. When your father died, it was so unexpected I couldn't deal with it."

"I remember—all of us were struggling," Blake said with his own painful flashback.

"You were away at school; I just didn't want to walk into the study and see his things. So, I hired movers to box everything and put it all in the attic."

"How much is there?"

"A lot. But I think I can help. The movers didn't box the book stuff."

"What do you mean?"

"Dad did that himself. He had a special box—for years, it sat in the corner of his office."

"Will you know which one it is?"

"Let's go find out."

The two made their way to the pull-down steps leading to the attic. The springs on the steps creaked as Blake pulled on the ring. He went up first, found the light switch, and called his mother. In the back corner of the attic, they found at least a hundred boxes.

"Okay, how are we going to find *the* box?"

"Look for one that looks different," his mom said.

"You're right, all the boxes look the same—from the movers, I guess."

Slowly, they began to move boxes, occasionally looking to see what treasure might lie in wait—mostly papers. Blake was reminded his dad grew up in an era before digital storage became the norm.

After a few minutes, they spotted a box that looked different. It was slightly smaller and visibly older than the others.

"Mom, is this it?" Blake asked, holding the box closer to the single light bulb illuminating their search-and-rescue effort. "What are these letters on the side of the box—NHH?"

"I don't know. I never noticed them before," she said.

"Let's take it downstairs and see what we have," Blake said.

After they descended to the kitchen, Blake looked at the box, wondering what he would find inside. His current challenges aside, this was his dad's work—a chance to learn from him, something Blake had longed for since the day his dad passed away.

His mother broke the silence: "Are you ready to open it?" She began to cry.

"What's wrong? Mom, are you okay?"

"No, I'm not. Your dad loved me and you with all his life, but he loved his people, too. He wanted to serve them. He struggled with how to do that well. That's why he started putting things in this box." She spoke through her tears. "The week before he died, he told me he was ready."

"Ready for what?"

"Ready to write the book! All the years of our marriage he had been searching, striving, and seeking. For a long time, he felt he was looking for one final piece, something that would make the picture complete. Whatever it was, the last piece of the puzzle, he finally found it—he was ready . . . he was so excited, as excited as I had ever seen him since the day you were born. He found what he was looking for, and then he died."

Through her tears, she looked at Blake. "Who knows? Maybe you can write the book."

"Me? Mom, have you lost your mind? I'm not the guy. I'm really struggling just to lead my organization. I don't need to write a book—I need to read one!"

"Hopefully, the answers you need will be in this box," she said.

Blake opened the box, and they both peered in. Not knowing what to expect, they were both underwhelmed—no beam of light, no chorus of angels, nothing—just a box of papers, notes, photos, maps, and clippings from magazines and newspapers. There were also a couple of paperback books, one on the civil rights movement and another on Renaissance art. At first glance, it was an odd mix of artifacts with no apparent system at all—no file folders or rubber bands holding items together. Honestly, it was a mess. They just looked at each other.

"I guess this is what a book looks like before it becomes a book," she said.

They both laughed.

Blake gave his mom a big, long hug. "I miss him," she said as they embraced.

"Me, too," he said as a tear rolled down his cheek.

Clues

When Blake returned home, the first thing he did was show Megan the box. She loved mysteries, and he invited her to help him solve this one. Although they didn't have a study like his dad, they did have a basement. Blake and Megan decided to set up there and organize all the pieces on the wall, like the police detectives they had seen on television. This would allow them to look for connections and see any patterns that might emerge. They could group like items and perhaps get inside Jeff's brain. Since Clint was at work and Kristen was at a friend's house, they decided to jump right in.

After about an hour, the patterns were still elusive. The only system they could discern was a color coding his dad had used—pale blue, lime green, bright yellow, and neon orange highlighters. And because only a very small percentage of the hundreds of items were color coded, it appeared as though Jeff had been trying to shroud the truth. Then, there was the cryptic NHH on the side of the box. Nothing they found hinted at the letters' meaning.

"Here's a scrap of paper with some numbers on it and the letters B O B. There is one thing different about this one," Megan said. "It also has a red circle and an exclamation mark. I haven't seen other circles yet."

"Let's keep it separate," Blake suggested, "and see if other red circles appear. Here's a picture of us on vacation. I must have been twelve years old."

"Where was it taken?" Megan asked.

"I think the sign in the back says Selma."

"Where is that?"

"Alabama, I think."

"Okay, hold on—that may be our first real clue . . ."

"Why would you say that?"

"There are two books in this box."

"Right."

"One is about the civil rights movement. Let me look." Megan quickly began to flip through the pages. "Here!"

"What?"

"A red circle on the section about Selma!" she said excitedly.

"What does it say?"

"It's an account of Bloody Sunday."

"I've never heard of it," Blake said.

"Me either, but it says here that in 1965, the civil rights movement began to gain traction in an unlikely place—the Edmund Pettus Bridge."

Megan continued and read aloud a portion of the account of that fateful day. When she finished, they just looked at each other.

"Megan, are you thinking what I'm thinking?"

"Want to go to Alabama?" she said, beating him to the punch.

"Sure."

"I have an idea: let's both read this book, and I'll do some additional research before we go," Megan suggested.

"Okay, I'll brief Charles and the team on what we found and what we're about to do. I know the whole thing is crazy, but I feel like I need to tell them something."

~

Over the next week, they made arrangements for the kids, rescheduled a dentist appointment, and found a day Blake could be out of the office. Blake met with Charles and the team to tell them about the box and his travel plans.

On the morning of the big trip, Blake greeted Megan with his usual question as she ambled into the kitchen. "Sleep well?"

"As well as possible when we have to get up so early."

"Honey, it's 8:00."

"I know, but I'm willing to sacrifice precious sleep to solve our mystery." She smiled as Blake handed her a cup of coffee.

During the drive to the airport, Megan said, "Okay, what exactly are we looking for in Selma?"

"That's a really good question. I've been thinking about it from my dad's point of view."

"And what was he looking for?"

"Well, I think he was trying to discover what causes or contributes to high levels of engagement. And as I think about all that's happening at work, lack of engagement may be the single most important factor limiting our success today."

"I didn't know it was that big a deal," Megan said.

"In our business, and in virtually all organizations, engagement can be the game changer. If we have a lofty vision, noble goals, compelling values—even outstanding products, services, and systems to deliver them—but our people aren't fully engaged, we suboptimize everything. It's virtually impossible to maintain a competitive advantage without engaged people," Blake said.

"And if engagement is low, you also have tremendous untapped potential," Megan added.

"We might have more untapped potential than most."

"Why is that?" she asked.

"We've selected the most outstanding people in our industry. Think of it as a garage full of the fastest cars in the world. Engagement is like the gas for the engines. Without the fuel, all that horsepower and potential just sits there."

It's virtually impossible to maintain a competitive advantage without engaged people.

"So, tell me again why we're going to Selma," Megan smiled.

"We're looking for what Dad was looking for."

"Gasoline for the engines?" Megan quipped.

"You're close—we're trying to figure out how to help our people care more."

A few moments later Megan added, "I've arranged for us to talk to Sandra Fleming in Selma—she's the woman who wrote the book."

"Wonderful! I want to hear her story firsthand."

Selma

When Blake and Megan landed in Montgomery, they still had about an hour drive before they would arrive in Selma.

"How old was Sandra in 1965?" Blake wondered out loud.

"She was ten," Megan responded.

"I want to hear what happened and why she believes people were willing to be part of the struggle," Blake said.

When the couple drove into Selma, they went directly to the bridge, where Sandra said she would be waiting.

"Sandra?" Blake said tentatively.

"Yes. You must be Blake and Megan. Welcome to Selma," she said with a warm smile and a lovely Southern accent.

"Yes. Thanks for meeting us here today. We loved your book."

"It was a labor of love. You may have noticed, I dedicated it to my mom. She was my hero and my inspiration. We marched together across this bridge, and I didn't want our story to be lost in the wake of history."

"We'd love to learn more. Is there a café nearby?"

"Oh yes, and we have some of the best pie in Alabama just around the corner. Follow me."

"Should we drive?" Blake asked.

"No, we're not going far. Besides, I want you to walk across the bridge."

As the three walked across the bridge, no one said a word. Blake and Megan were thinking about what happened there over fifty years ago. Sandra, as she had thousands of times before, drew silent strength from those who had walked before her.

In the café, time had stood still. It was 1965, or at least what the couple thought it would have been like—from the linoleum floor tiles to the Naugahyde barstools and the purring of the milkshake machine. While Megan and Blake were soaking it all in, the waitress, in her period-perfect uniform, apron and all, approached the table with a warm welcome and menus.

"No, thank you," Sandra said. "No menus needed; we only have one question for you: What kind of pies has Clare made today?"

"Peach and pecan," the waitress said.

"You can't go wrong with either one," Sandra said to her new friends. "If I'm right, the peaches and the pecans came from the trees just outside of town. You'll never have pie fresher or tastier than this," Sandra added with a note of hometown pride.

Blake ordered the pecan and Megan chose the peach. "Thanks again for meeting with us," Megan said.

"Delighted," Sandra said. "Exactly how can I serve you?"

"Can you tell us what happened here in 1965? And then, we would love to know why you think so many people were willing to march. What compelled you and others to take a stand—why did those courageous women and men care so much?"

"Let's begin with the story itself . . .

"On March 7, my mama and I were up early to go to church. When we arrived, we were told we were going to march to Montgomery. It was intended to be a nonviolent protest to support African Americans' right to vote. Little did we know the day would be remembered as Bloody Sunday."

"That's a long walk!" Megan interjected.

"Yes, fifty-one miles. I'm not sure anyone had considered all the implications; I know we had not, but the energy was high . . . we were going to march! As we approached the midpoint on the bridge, we could see the troopers on the other side, but many in our group were naïve; we thought, surely they would part to let us through. We were shocked by their response."

"What happened?" Megan asked.

"They advanced to meet us, hitting people with clubs and hurling tear gas canisters at us. It became obvious that we were not going to march to Montgomery—at least not that day. I tried to stay really close to Mama during the chaos that ensued. Some ran, some fell, others were knocked down. We made it back to the other side; I remember clutching my mama's skirt as we ran. I was so scared and thankful when we made it home—alive."

"Unbelievable—and you were there!" Blake said. "I know you were young, but since then you've researched, relived, and retold the story countless times. Can you help us understand why people would care enough to be so bold?"

"Well, I guess others might give you a different answer, but as a self-proclaimed historian," she smiled, "let me tell you what I think. A couple of things probably emboldened the people on the bridge that day and in the larger civil rights movement.

"The cause was just. When you are on the right side of an issue, you can draw strength from that. We knew the jury of history was watching. We decided to stand up and make a difference.

"We also had gifted leadership. Dr. King inspired us to do the right thing—even when it was hard. But make no mistake: it was never about him—it was about all men . . . and women," she smiled.

"We didn't feel alone in our efforts; we felt the support of free people around the world. There is power, value, and tremendous strength in connection . . . to the cause and with others. We marched with family and friends, coworkers and neighbors. Even the strangers among us felt like they belonged.

"Like an old quilt my mama made years ago, the individual pieces may not look like much, but when you stitch them together, you can create something beautiful. We were stitched together—we were connected; we were stronger together. This is where the strength to march came from . . . in my humble opinion."

Like an old quilt my mama made years ago, the individual pieces may not look like much, but when you stitch them together, you can create something beautiful.

For the better part of the afternoon, Blake and Megan asked a lot of questions about Sandra's mom, the rest of her family, her life since Bloody Sunday, her plans for future books, and more. They also enjoyed some delicious pie.

"Thank you for your time and your insight. This has been a day we'll never forget," Blake said.

"And, if you find yourself in our part of the world, you always have a place to stay," Megan added.

As they walked back on to the street, Sandra gave them a hug.

"Aren't you going with us?"

"No, my house is the other direction. Besides, I want to let you walk the bridge one more time. Travel safe."

Twelve-hundred forty-eight feet across the bridge—with each step, Blake and Megan tried to imagine the emotions of Sandra and her friends. The images from more than fifty years ago flashed fresh across their minds.

When they were back at their car, Megan said, "I think we have the first piece of your dad's puzzle. **Connection** is huge, if people are disconnected from a cause or each other, it would be extremely difficult to care deeply."

"I agree."

The fifty-one-mile drive back to Montgomery was quiet.

Next

When Blake and Megan returned home, they were energized. The trip to Selma had been both fun and informative.

"That was so helpful, I think we may need to take a few more trips," Megan said with a big smile.

"I agree," Blake said. "But where should we go?"

"Are you ready for our next clue, Inspector?" she said.

"Can hardly wait, but can we eat first? The food on the plane was . . . well, you know."

"I'll set a card table in the basement. We can have a working dinner." Megan smiled.

"Where are the kids?" Blake asked.

"Kristen is studying with Becky, and Clint was going to a movie after his team finishes practice."

When the two entered the basement, Blake was once again struck by the enormity of their project. The wall looked like something you would see on the big screen. It was ten feet wide and almost six feet high. He and Megan had reviewed every scrap of paper. Some were nothing more than fragments—receipts from shops and restaurants, random names and numbers. Thankfully, the color coding helped some. And the red circles might turn out to be important clues. The first circle had tipped the scales toward Selma—based on how informative that trip had been, they would pay special attention to the others.

All the articles, photos, maps, and notes had been organized into groups—five in all. Actually, four plus a very small fifth category with just one small note. Then, there was the bonus pool—not really a category at all, but it contained the items about which Blake and Megan had no idea.

The four main categories were separated by colored yarn—a technique Megan copied from a detective novel. The colors added a nice sense of whimsy to the board.

Above one column, Megan wrote the word Connection, based on their insights from Selma. This new clarity also allowed her to move several items into this column. Hopefully, additional trips would help them sort more of the material.

"Incredible!" Blake said. "This represents years of my dad's life and leadership. In some ways, I feel like I have the opportunity to spend time with him again."

"I know." Megan took Blake's hand while they stood there staring at the board.

"Let's eat," Blake said.

Megan turned and made a grand gesture toward the card table with its checkered cloth and a box of pizza unceremoniously placed in the center. "I had pizza delivered!"

As they sat on folding chairs eating their pizza, Blake looked at the big board and asked, "What's next?"

"We have some choices . . . Where do you want to go first: Wisconsin, Italy, or Greece?"

"Slow down . . . seriously?" Blake said with a chuckle. "Is this a thinly veiled attempt to take a vacation?"

"No! But that appears to be what your dad did with you guys. Was it so bad?"

This represents years of my dad's life and leadership. In some ways, I feel like I have the opportunity to spend time with him again.

"It wasn't bad—it was a little weird. Other kids went to the beach . . . a trip to Selma needed more explanation than I could offer my friends as a child," Blake laughed.

"Well, we don't have to take the kids, but we are probably going to need to travel," Megan suggested.

"What led you to this conclusion?"

"Interestingly enough, your dad did not include *any* category labels or titles. But the combination of the color coding and the red circles does suggest several destinations. Here's the bottom line: There is only one place circled in each group. And in the case of Pella, it's actually circled on a map."

"Where's Pella?" Blake asked.

"Greece," Megan said.

"Only four circles in all this stuff?"

"Well, not exactly. There is a fifth circle, and it's a true mystery."

"Like the rest of this is not . . ."

"I hear you, but do you see the sparsely populated fifth column on the board?"

"Yeah, I was going to ask you about that. It only contains a small scrap of paper—no color to help place it, just a red circle . . . with an exclamation mark. Remind me, what's on the paper?"

"I'm not sure exactly. The letters B O B and some numbers—maybe a phone number, maybe a partial address, I don't know," Megan said.

"That's really cryptic; I like putting it in its own category. We can label that column 'Strange.'"

"Call it whatever you like for now; where do you want to go next? Do you agree we should travel?" The truth was, Megan loved to travel, but between their schedules and the kids, opportunities had been limited for the last few years.

"Where do we go?" Blake asked.

"I told you already—you've got to keep up." This jab came with a big grin. "We have three choices: Wisconsin, Italy, or Greece."

"I thought you were kidding."

"Nope—dead serious."

"What are we looking for—exactly?" Blake asked politely.

"The same thing we were looking for in Selma—clues, insights, ideas, anything to point to our bigger question: How do we help people care more? How do we raise their level of engagement?

"Now, back to the plan," Megan continued. "I suggest we go to Europe first. After we return, we can do a short trip to Wisconsin."

"Green Bay, I hope," Blake said. "I've always wanted to go to a game there."

"I'll tell you more later," Megan teased.

The next part of the conversation centered on exactly where they would go and whom they would try to meet on their European tour. Admittedly, the clues were thin for both of these trips, but at least they could have some time away. They decided this would be an adults-only trip. Blake would call his mom about helping with the kids.

Florence

Of all the places Blake and Megan would visit, this was by far the biggest stretch. Here's what they had for clues: a book about Renaissance art with the title circled in red and about twenty-five different articles and individual handwritten notes with some color coding but seemingly disparate content. Regardless, Megan was secretly giddy; well, maybe not so secretly—she had always wanted to visit Italy.

Because the book was about art, they decided to begin their visit with a trip to the more prominent museums. And to learn more, they hired Maria, a docent from a local university, to serve as their guide. During their brief visit, they would see both Florence and Rome—a short train ride separated the two cities. Maria had agreed to accompany them.

Maria met the couple at the airport. She was a tall, well-dressed, middle-aged woman with long brown hair. Her educational resume was stunning—a PhD in Renaissance history and two undergraduate degrees in sociology and art history. She was definitely the right person to give Blake and Megan a deep dive into the history and implications of the Renaissance.

"Welcome to Italy!" she said, beaming.

"Thank you!" Blake said. "We are thrilled to be with you. This is my wife, Megan."

Megan said a few words in Italian. Maria responded in her native language.

"Okay, you guys—cut it out. Megan is just showing off. She studied Italian in college."

"Only one semester; I just used all my skills to offer that greeting. But it's fun to try it again," Megan said.

Maria responded to Megan, again in Italian.

"English. We need to speak English. Sorry, ladies, that's all I've got," Blake said.

"Gladly," Maria smiled at Megan. "Please tell me again what you hope to learn while you are here. Your message was a bit unclear to me."

"Sorry about that, but we are not totally clear on that ourselves. Can we talk while we drive to our hotel?"

"Certainly. The car is waiting."

As they drove, Megan opened the conversation: "Before we talk about our agenda, tell us about you."

Maria shared her story and her deep passion for her country, the people, and their heritage. "It's why I do what I do," she said.

Blake and Megan told their story and why they had been willing to travel so far with such little information. "We're trying to solve a mystery," Megan said. "At the highest level, we want to know how Blake and other leaders can help people care more at work. And more specifically, how does Renaissance art figure into the answer?"

"Let's begin with the art," Maria said. "We have sculptures, architecture, paintings, drawings, frescoes, tapestries, and more from the Renaissance period."

"Hold on," Blake said. "Give us a little more context; I think I dozed off a few times in my art history classes. And as I prepared for this trip, I realized the dates for the period vary depending on who you are asking. From your perspective, when was the Renaissance?"

"The Renaissance was a period between the Middle Ages and the modern era, generally agreed to be between 1350 and 1600 AD. However, you are correct: some scholars insist it ended when Rome fell in 1527, a technicality as far as I'm concerned. I don't think a movement like the Renaissance has a hard stop on any given date. The influences ripple even to this day."

Blake turned to Megan and said with a smile, "I think we have the right guide."

"What does it mean—the word *renaissance*?" Megan asked.

"Rebirth—a new way to think and see the world. A fresh wind began to blow in Florence and eventually spread throughout Europe. Art, science, literature, astronomy, exploration, philosophy, and religion were reborn during this period. Even learning and communication were impacted with the invention of moveable type. Virtually no facet of life was left untouched by this period of history. The Renaissance brought new life and vitality to every corner of Europe. If you're ready, we can let the creators of the Renaissance speak for themselves!" Maria said.

The next three days were spectacular. For both Megan and Blake, many of their college memories of sitting in dark rooms looking at lifeless images in art history classes were shattered. What they saw was stunning—the Sistine Chapel, the statue of David, works by Leonardo da Vinci, Raphael, and much, much more.

Exhausted and exhilarated, the travelers concluded their whirlwind tour.

"Let's go to dinner and try to make sense of it all," Blake suggested.

"I know the perfect place to end this chapter of your journey. I'll make reservations. Let's meet in the lobby in an hour," Maria said.

The restaurant was picture-perfect and quintessentially Italian—all the way to the white tablecloths on the street-side tables illuminated by candlelight.

"Thanks for recommending this place—it is beautiful," Megan said.

"Yes, but the best part is the food!" Maria assured them.

During dinner, Blake was eager to find the insight from their experience. He was still rolling the same question over and over in his mind: *What does all of this have to do with engagement?*

"Maria, I have a question: What caused the Renaissance?" Blake asked.

"That is a question many of my colleagues at the university have spent their lives debating." Maria offered a faint smile to suggest she too had thought about this question. "I have my own theory," she began, "but before I offer it, why do you ask?"

"I'm not sure . . ." Blake hesitated. "I just wonder if the factors that led to this world-changing movement may also be relevant when leaders think about how to better engage their workforce."

"Tell me more," Maria said.

"I don't know; it's just hard to wrap my head around what caused all of this to happen. I don't want to believe it was the product of chance. Obviously, the artists cared deeply about their work. You couldn't create the things we've seen with a casual or indifferent attitude. The passion was evident in everything we saw."

"Yes, I agree. For most of the artists, their work represented their livelihood and reputation; art was their vocation, and for many, their calling. Some would say, passion was the ethos of the era," Maria said.

"Can you say a little more about the passion?" Megan asked.

"Sure. From my point of view, passion was a defining characteristic of the period. Consider Galileo. His views landed him under house arrest for the last eleven years of his life, yet he wouldn't recant. Or Martin Luther. His beliefs found him excommunicated by the church. These were not casual contributors, and there were many others. Without their passion and conviction, they would not have changed the world."

"Okay, you're making my point; these people obviously cared . . . Passion is caring on steroids. Why did they care so much? That is *the* question."

"Here's my theory on the catalyst for the Renaissance period," Maria began. "There was not a *single* causal factor; there were many elements that converged to create this cultural phenomenon—a combination of the right people, high levels of interaction and collaboration, physical proximity, and resources—"

Megan interrupted, "What kind of resources?"

"Primarily money," Maria said.

"Yes, I read something about wealthy families. I think one of them was named Medici; is that correct?" Blake asked.

"Yes," Maria said. "They were some of the most generous patrons of the day. Their family commissioned many works by many artists. However, resources were also provided by countless others. Even the church got in on the action; that's why Michelangelo agreed to paint the ceiling of the Sistine Chapel—Pope Julius II was a well-funded and persuasive client."

"Any other contributing factors?" Blake asked.

"Yes, I was about to say, one other major element served as fuel on the fire of the rebirth: the mindset," Maria said.

"I'm not sure what to do with that one," Megan said.

"Coming out of decades of famine and disease sometimes appropriately called the Dark Ages, people had an openness to new ideas, a spirit of innovation, a willingness to try new things and challenge existing conventions. It was a wonderful dynamic. This renaissance mindset ultimately swept the region and then the continent."

"Which came first?" Blake asked. "The elements you described or the mindset that fueled the movement?"

"The interplay between the people and the elements, driven by the mindset, enabled the rebirth to create its own energy," Maria said. "All factors were critical, but it cannot be reduced to a formula. There was certainly some magic in the mix."

"How would you summarize all of that?" Megan asked.

"What causes the rain? The combination of multiple elements: humidity, temperature, wind speed and direction, etcetera. The more ideal the conditions, the bigger the storm. The conditions were perfect for the Renaissance," Maria suggested.

"What a powerful summary. If we want people to genuinely care deeply, like the artists, thinkers, craftspeople, theologians, and musicians of the Renaissance, we have to create the right **Environment**," Blake said.

The interplay between the people and the elements, driven by the mindset, enabled the rebirth to create its own energy.

"I think that's right. Now, we can have a debate another time about the relative weight of the various elements, but remove any one of them and I think you create a different and diminished impact."

Blake turned to Megan and said, "This is so helpful. It also explains something we've been wondering about."

"What's that?" Megan asked.

"Many of the articles, clippings, and notes Dad had amassed didn't make sense to us. I remember we even said they looked 'random.' We were looking at the pieces, not the big picture. The list of factors Maria just shared might look random too, but if you step back, they create the context or the environment for extraordinary things."

"And extreme levels of care," Megan added.

"Our challenge will be to identify the modern elements—the catalyst for our own caring Renaissance," Blake said. "I'll ask the team for their help as soon as we return home."

Pella

During the flight to Thessaloniki, Blake and Megan reviewed their notes. The threads that connected them to the ancient city were not much more than they had for their last stop and in some ways, less; there was no book on ancient Greek art or culture. However, they had found a map with the city of Pella circled. Based on what they had learned in Selma and Florence, this was encouraging. Also, they had a photo of a marble bust of someone they assumed to be Alexander the Great. A little fact-checking led them to discover that not only was Pella the birthplace of Alexander, but the government had built a museum there largely to memorialize his accomplishments.

Once again, they had prearranged for a guide and driver to meet them at the airport. Their experiences with Maria and Sandra had been so helpful, they hoped their time with Gamal would be the same. The handwritten sign he held high was an easy find in the crowded arrival hall.

"Welcome to Greece! Is this your first visit?"

"Yes, for both of us," Blake said.

"Please tell me again what you want to see. Your email mentioned only one place—the museum in Pella. Is that all?"

"Well, we think so . . ." Megan said hesitantly. "We'll tell you more on the way."

Gamal listened intently to the account of Blake and Megan's journey thus far, including the objective of their search. He nodded politely but clearly thought the couple was suffering from jet lag—or worse!

Sensing his unspoken conclusion, Blake said, "I know this sounds crazy—it is crazy! It's not rational at any level. However, Megan and I are long overdue for some time together, we love to travel, and the work my father started matters. I need to finish his journey . . . for me and my organization."

"Okay, we'll be in Pella soon. Do you want to go to your hotel?"

"Will the museum still be open this afternoon when we arrive?"

"Yes. For about an hour," Gamal said.

"Let's start there. If we don't find what we are looking for, we'll return tomorrow."

"Again," Gamal asked, "exactly what are we looking for?"

"We're not sure."

"Just as I thought," Gamal mumbled under his breath. "Crazy Americans!"

"However, we know Alexander was a fantastic leader."

"Yes," Gamal said. "One of the best in the history of the world."

"For him to be so successful as a leader, we're betting his people really cared. We need to discover why they cared so deeply," Megan said.

"From the grave, Alexander will speak," Gamal said as they arrived at the museum.

Upon entering, Blake and Megan both realized they would need more than an hour to survey all that lay before them—there were many, many artifacts along with a seemingly endless number of placards providing information regarding the items on display. Undaunted, the couple jumped right in.

After their hour was up, they agreed to meet Gamal at their hotel the next morning to continue their search. Over dinner, Blake and Megan decided to review their notes.

"I must have missed a few days of class during my ancient history courses," Megan began.

"What makes you say that?"

"Based on our quick visit to the museum this afternoon, I can tell you I knew virtually nothing about Alexander."

"I don't know much either," Blake said. "What have we learned so far that might be helpful?"

"He was tutored by Aristotle, who was tutored by Plato, who was tutored by Socrates," Megan said.

"Interesting. What does that tell you about why his army appeared to care so much?"

"Nothing. I just thought it was interesting," Megan smiled playfully.

"Okay, thanks—I may have something a little more on point," Blake said, returning the smile.

"Alexander made it his practice to visit the wounded after a battle and ask them to tell him their stories," Blake added.

"That's nice," Megan said.

"No, not nice . . . Here's the point: he would then go and tell the stories of courage and bravery to the other men."

"I'm guessing that fired up the troops."

"I would think so," Blake said.

"Anything else?" Megan asked.

"Probably. Let's get a good night's sleep and see what we can find tomorrow."

~

The next morning Blake, Megan, and Gamal were at the door when the museum opened.

"Gamal, based on our short visit last night, it appears as though Alexander really cared for his men. He didn't just *say* he cared; he showed them with his actions."

"Follow me." Gamal took them into another room featuring the battles Alexander and his men fought, undefeated for fifteen years!

"Look over here at this display chronicling Alexander's wounds; eight times, he was injured in battle, from a cleaver to the head, which split his helmet, to an arrow that pierced his lung after he jumped off the top of a wall into enemy forces.

"He didn't just tell his men their cause was just and their struggle worth their willing sacrifice—he fought beside them time and time again," Gamal said.

He didn't just tell his men their cause was just and their struggle worth their willing sacrifice—he fought beside them time and time again.

"I'm guessing this contributed significantly to the engagement of his men," Blake said.

"Okay, let's connect the dots," Megan said. "I think **Affirmation** is the theme we've been looking for. Alexander affirmed the courage of the wounded, the worth of every man under his command, and was even willing to share their struggles in battle," Megan said.

"He affirmed them with word and deed," Gamal offered with a note of pride in his voice. "He was a renowned strategist and warrior, but he was also a leader who knew his success ultimately rested with his army. He did everything he could to win their hearts."

Interesting choice of words, Blake thought. "Thanks, Gamal, I think we've learned what we needed here. We're going to the coast to enjoy more of your country before we return to the States."

Eight Digits

After returning home, Blake and Megan were feeling the effects of their trip across the world. It would be a few days before they would meet to review the big board and plan the next leg of their adventure. However, Blake used this break to brief the team on their findings thus far.

"It has been amazing!" Blake said to the team.

"In Selma, we believe the chief insight was Connection. We're still pulling it all together, but we think this is a big idea," Blake said. "In Florence, we were struck by the power of creating the right Environment for people to thrive and care to blossom. Finally, in Pella—"

Gary interrupted, "Excuse me . . . where is Pella?"

"Greece," Blake said. "I didn't know where it was either," he smiled.

"And why Pella?" Rose asked.

"It's the birthplace of Alexander the Great. They have a museum there to tell his story and preserve his legacy."

"What did you learn there?" Charles asked.

"We think Alexander was an outstanding leader with many strengths, but as it relates to this work, we're convinced Affirmation was a key to the engagement of his men."

The team asked a lot of questions—they wanted more details. Blake did his best to answer them but admitted these ideas were still in their formative state.

"Megan and I still have a trip or two before us. I will report back shortly, and then we'll examine all the pieces and see if we can put this puzzle together."

~

"Are you ready for our next trip?" Blake said as soon as he walked in the door.

"Well, aren't you full of energy?" Megan observed. "What happened to your jet lag?"

"Talking with the team today fired me up. I'm ready to go—are you?"

"Absolutely! How about tonight after dinner we go down and look at the board? I really haven't had any breakthroughs, but I'll be happy to share what I've been thinking."

Later that evening when Blake walked downstairs and turned the corner, he saw the board for the first time since their return; Megan had clearly understated her progress! The board appeared to be more orderly, and the patterns were becoming sharper.

"Wow! You have been busy. Tell me what you've done."

"Not much. I really just did two things. I labeled the groupings: Connection, Environment, and Affirmation."

"That really helped. But it looks like you did something else," Blake commented.

"Yes, as you recall, there were only a few items color coded."

"Yeah, that's how we determined the big buckets."

"Correct. But here's what is different on the board now . . . I took all the non-color-coded artifacts and tried to place them under one of the now labeled themes. I was able to place about 50 percent of the unmarked items: an article on recognition under Affirmation, a team photo under Connection, two articles on collaboration I put in the Environment column, etcetera. That's why the board looks more complete; I guess it is." Megan beamed as if she had been working on a crossword puzzle and discovered an eleven-letter word for *rebirth*.

"Fantastic! Any additional insights?"

"No, I'm afraid not. I do have a question we need to answer," Megan said.

"What's that?"

"I know we're going to Wisconsin next week, but that still leaves the final destination unidentified."

"*If* there is a final destination," Blake added.

"I think there is. Let's try to figure this out . . ."

For what felt like an hour, the two sat thinking about what the cryptic message on the small tattered piece of paper might mean.

"Should we forget it and focus on what we have?" Blake said.

"No, I don't think so."

"Why not?"

"There is something different about this note."

"What? It's just a bunch of numbers and a few letters scribbled on a piece of paper."

"No, you missed two major clues," Megan insisted. "One, it has a red circle; all the other circles have represented destinations."

"Okay, I knew that. What else?

"It has an exclamation point."

"So?"

"I don't know. I just think it must be significant," Megan said.

Blake looked at her and the note. "Let's keep thinking. What do we know?"

"It is an eight-digit number."

"Anything else?" Blake asked.

"The letters B O B are written underneath it."

"What could the letters be?"

"An abbreviation, I'm assuming. Notice the spacing between the letters, and it's written in all caps," Megan said.

"No, I think it's a name. It just hit me: Dad always wrote in all caps," Blake said.

"Okay, maybe it is a name. What is the number? We can assume it is not a Social Security number—they are nine digits."

"Not a passport number—nine digits," Blake said.

"Not a phone number—seven or ten digits," Megan added.

"Not a zip code or an area code," Blake said.

"Maybe a driver's license number—some states do use eight digits. But let's hope that's not it—way too hard to track down," Megan said, shaking her head.

"Based on what we've experienced so far, Dad was looking back in history for timeless principles—that's how we ended up in Selma, Florence, and Pella. Let's think of the number in that context."

"What context? An old number?" Megan whacked Blake on the arm.

"No, I'm serious. Have you checked the National Register of Historic Places?" Blake asked.

"No, can't say I have." Megan smirked, pulling out her laptop. She found the site and typed in the eight-digit reference number and stared in disbelief at the screen.

"What? Did you find something?" Blake asked.

"I think we're going to Texas."

"What's in Texas?" Blake asked.

"A ranch . . . a very old ranch. Want to know its name?"

"No, just keep it a surprise." Blake paused and then said, "Of course, I want to know!"

"NHH Ranch."

"Those are the letters on the outside of Dad's box! What else does it say?"

"The original owner was named Robert Conroy."

"Could he be our Bob?"

"Probably not; Robert is listed as the owner of the property in 1794," she smiled. "Let's buy a ticket. As soon as we get back from Wisconsin, we can focus on finding someone who knows Bob's story."

"Outstanding!" Blake said.

"I just have one question," Megan said. "How did you know the National Register of Historic Places used an eight-digit reference number?"

"Lucky guess," Blake smiled. "Let's go to Wisconsin!"

Green Bay

Of all the places in the world, Blake would not have dreamed of visiting Green Bay, Wisconsin, to learn about engagement. It was not on Megan's list of "Before I Die" destinations either. However, this was a slam dunk regarding their search. The clues for this stop were much more direct: they had a map with Green Bay circled, an article about the 1967 Ice Bowl, and the name Luther Gibbons. A quick Google search revealed that Luther had been on the field in 1967 as the groundskeeper for the Packers. Luther, now almost ninety, agreed to meet the couple at his home.

The address was on Shadow Lane, but Blake had no idea Luther actually lived in the shadow of Lambeau Field, the home of the Packers. As they pulled into the drive of the 1960s-style ranch home, Blake could feel his pulse racing. He had been a Packers fan for years—and so had his dad.

Luther graciously opened his home to the couple. They exchanged small talk for a few minutes. Luther shared how he landed his job with the Packers over sixty years ago. He told stories of Lombardi and other Packers legends. Blake was having the time of his life.

Megan, enjoying the company but not as mesmerized by the stories, wanted to learn whatever influenced Jeff to include Green Bay as a must-see destination. "Mr. Gibbons, can you tell us about the Ice Bowl?"

"I would love to . . . but I would rather tell that story on the field," Luther said.

"On the field?" Blake said. "Are you kidding me? We can go on the field?"

"If you would like to. I gave up my day job years ago, but I still have connections." Luther smiled like a kid who just pulled one over on his parents. "Let's go!"

The old man shuffled slowly across the room and through a doorway into his garage, the couple close behind. They found a golf cart charged and ready to go. "Hop in," he said, "I'll drive." Blake wasn't totally sure this was a good idea, but they were only going a couple of hundred yards across the street.

As they approached a gated entrance, the guard saw Luther coming, waved, and opened the gates so he didn't even have to slow down. "Thanks, Larry," Luther said as the cart sped through the entrance. In a moment, they were at the mouth of the tunnel opening onto the field.

"December 31, 1967," Luther began as the threesome walked toward the back of the end zone. "The NFL Championship Game—the winner would advance to Super Bowl II. The Packers were playing Tom Landry and the Dallas Cowboys. Vince Lombardi and his team had won the championship the two previous years. They wanted to make it three in a row."

"I guess it was cold," Megan said.

Blake looked at Megan. "It was the *Ice Bowl*."

"Yes, ma'am. If you call fifteen *below zero* cold—that was the temperature at kickoff, although it *really* got cold during the game." Luther smiled and shivered as he recalled the day. "And with the wind chill, it was *minus forty-eight degrees*."

Yes, ma'am. If you call fifteen *below zero* cold—that was the temperature at kickoff, although it *really* got cold during the game.

"I can't imagine," Blake said.

"Hard to explain. So cold, one official almost bled to death," Luther chuckled.

"Really? What happened?" Megan was trying to connect frigid cold with bleeding.

"Well, not really, but he did require some first aid. His whistle stuck to his lips, and when he pulled it away, he pulled the skin off—blood was everywhere. I can still see it like it was yesterday," Luther said with a twinkle in his eyes.

"Other than being so cold, why was the game memorable?" Megan asked.

"Well, remember, it was the championship . . . and the Cowboys versus the Packers is always a big deal," Luther added.

"Anything else?" Blake asked.

"Well, the ending was right out of the movies," Luther mused.

"Tell us."

"It was third down, and the Packers had the ball on the two-foot line with sixteen seconds to go; they were behind by three, seventeen to fourteen. The Packers called a time-out, their last. Bart Starr, the future Hall of Fame quarterback, and Lombardi met on the sidelines. What happened next was extraordinary."

"What happened?" Megan asked.

"Starr called his own number. He told the coach he wanted to run the ball himself."

"Why was that extraordinary?" Megan was confused.

"It depends on your perspective. Think about the context and the potential consequences," Luther said. "It was third down, no more time-outs, and if this play failed, no time to get the field goal team on the field for the tie . . ."

"Unless," Blake added, "you threw a pass. Then, if it was incomplete, you would have time for the kick."

"That's what the Cowboys thought. No way were they expecting a run, much less a quarterback sneak; Starr had not done a sneak all year long!"

"What happened next?" Megan was beginning to understand the magnitude of the moment.

"The extraordinary part . . . Lombardi let Starr do it! He gave him the ball and the responsibility for the championship. It took tremendous leadership courage from Starr and Lombardi to call that play.

"And, as they say, the rest is history. Starr ran the play, scored, and won the championship. It was mayhem around here. We all knew we had just witnessed a game that would be talked about for generations—and not just because it was cold." Luther told the story as if he could still *feel* the roar of the crowd. "You know, the Packers went on to win the Super Bowl—it all came down to that play."

"It was a remarkable sequence of events. Thanks for being our guide today. Let's head back to your house," Blake suggested.

As they made the short ride back to Luther's house, the sunset began to usher in the cool night air, although this did nothing to chill Blake's enthusiasm; he believed they had just discovered another key contributor to increased engagement.

As they said their good-byes, Luther said, "I have something for you." He went to a drawer and pulled out a black and white photo and handed it to Blake. It was a photo of Bart Starr, under center, looking across the line, his breath and likeness literally frozen in time. It was the play they had just discussed! "I want you to have this."

"Really?"

"Sure. I've got no one else to give it to, and you seem like nice young people. And this way, you'll have something to remember me by," he grinned. "That's me in the background." He pointed to a slightly out of focus and grainy image of a much younger man watching history unfold on one very cold day in December 1967.

~

On the drive back to the airport, Blake was speechless. He finally got out the words "What a day!"

"It was really fun," Megan said, although Blake knew she didn't fully appreciate what he had just experienced. "And I'm glad he gave you that picture."

"Me too."

"So . . ." Megan continued, "did we learn what we came to learn?"

"I think we did."

"What is it? To tell you the truth, I got lost in the story."

"I think a key driver for engagement and genuine care is **Responsibility**."

"How do you figure that?"

"Lombardi was a genius, one of the best coaches who has ever lived. When Starr suggested the quarterback sneak, Lombardi could have said, 'No, Bart, I appreciate your initiative, your desire, and your passion, but I'm the coach; your idea makes no sense. Here's what we're going to do.' And you know what would have happened?"

"What?"

I think a key driver for engagement and genuine care is Responsibility.

"Starr would have run any play the coach called. However, that's not what happened. The coach let him decide. He gave him real responsibility. I think about my own life and leadership. I am certainly willing to follow the lead of another, but when I think about the times my engagement has been at its peak, it was when I had been entrusted with real responsibility."

"I think you just said something important."

"What was that?" Blake asked.

"When you were *entrusted* with real responsibility . . . I don't think we can underestimate the trust that preceded the coach's decision."

"Point taken. A leader must build trust before she or he will be willing to give someone real responsibility, but I still think the key is responsibility. Trust becomes tangible when it is expressed in the form of real responsibility. I think it's our final driver of engagement."

"Maybe, maybe not. There's one more piece," Megan reminded Blake.

"What's that?"

"I don't know, but hopefully, we'll find out in Texas!"

Update

Before the trip to Texas, Blake wanted to provide another update to Charles and his team. He really wanted them to help him and the organization figure out how to bring the ideas they were discovering to life. During the team meeting, he told them about Luther.

"So, as it relates to engagement, we think the primary lesson from the Ice Bowl was the power of Responsibility. We still have one visit to go, but I'm not sure what else we will learn. Connection, Environment, Affirmation, and Responsibility feels like a strong recipe for care to me," Blake concluded.

"So, are we finished?" Ben asked.

"Not so fast!" Rose said with some energy in her voice. "I'm not sure we've really started."

"What do you mean?" Charles asked.

"I'm not totally sure," Rose said. "It just feels like something big is missing. These are great concepts, but we've got to help people understand what to do with them."

"I agree," Blake began. "Something is missing. What Megan and I have found appears to make sense. I think our next step is for you guys to help us decide *how* we can make these ideas come to life. What must we do to unleash the power of Connection, Environment, Affirmation, and Responsibility? If we answer this question, I am convinced we will create a stronger, more care-filled organization."

What must we do to unleash the power of Connection, Environment, Affirmation, and Responsibility?

"Maybe that's it," Rose said. "If we don't tell people how to do these things in the real world, all we'll have are some interesting anecdotes from the past."

"That's our challenge," Charles agreed. "We'll get back to you as soon as we have more thoughts."

"How soon?" Blake asked. "I owe the entire organization a report on our findings from the assessment and our response."

"Can you give us ten days to process what you've shared today?" Charles asked.

"Sounds good to me—thanks!"

Charles called a team meeting for later the same day to discuss their next steps.

"Thanks for adjusting your calendars to meet this afternoon," Charles said. "To begin, I am so thankful to have a CEO who deeply cares about engagement. I have to confess, I've worked places where this was not the case."

"Me too," Ben added. "The fact Blake cares is a huge deal."

"How do we tackle our assignment?" Peggy asked.

"If we're going to find out how to make these elements work in our culture, we are going to need some modern examples of these ideas in action," Kim suggested.

"Right. Let's face it—all of Blake's cases were historical," Peggy said.

"Nothing he talked about happened in my lifetime," Gary added.

"Right. But if Blake and Megan's discoveries are principle-based, they should be timeless," Kim said.

"So, exactly what are we looking for again?" Gary wanted to be sure he didn't misunderstand the assignment.

"I'll take it from here," Rose said. "Blake has proposed four factors that contribute to higher levels of engagement, or caring as we have defined it: Connection, Environment, Affirmation, and Responsibility. My suggestion is that we split up and look for some real examples. Then, we can try to figure out how they turn their aspirations into reality."

"Anybody have one of these you would like to explore?" Peggy asked.

The team quickly made the following assignments:

- *Connection—Peggy*
- *Environment—Kim, Gary*
- *Affirmation—Charles*
- *Responsibility—Rose, Ben*

"We'll meet next Monday to hear what you've learned," Charles said. "Have fun!"

Connection

The next morning, Peggy was eager to find her case study. The idea of Connection as a key factor in engagement made perfect sense to her; not only did it seem logical, it mirrored her personal experience. She felt connected to her work, her team, and the organization and believed this contributed significantly to her own level of care at work. All she had to do was find an example for the team. Surely it wouldn't be that difficult.

In her mind, she began to review all the places where she encountered people who appeared to care deeply about their work. On the way to the office, she stopped by the florist to pick up some flowers for a coworker who was retiring.

In the shop, she met Betty. She was professional, knowledgeable, courteous, attentive, and energetic—and she really appeared to care.

Maybe this would be a good case study, even though it's very different from our business. I wonder if Betty's engagement is merely a coincidence or the result of a bigger strategy, Peggy thought.

"I have a strange question for you—not about flowers."

"Okay," Betty said hesitantly.

"Are all the employees around here like you?"

"Well, I'm not sure how to answer that. We have a fairly diverse team—age, race, gender, experience. So, no, I guess they are not like me."

"Let me reframe the question . . . You are amazing."

"Thanks, I try." Betty blushed just a little.

"You seem to really care about me as a customer. Am I right?"

"I do."

"So, does everyone here care as much as you do? And if they do, how is that possible?" Peggy asked.

"Wow. That's a lot to process," Betty admitted. "But yes, everyone around here really does care."

"I would love to learn more. Can I buy you a cup of coffee during your break?"

"Sure, in about two hours," Betty smiled.

"I'll be back," Peggy said as she turned to leave—so excited about the pending conversation, she forgot to pick up her flowers.

~

Two hours later, Peggy returned.

"I knew you would be back," Betty said. "You forgot your flowers." Both women laughed.

"Yeah, I was preoccupied thinking about the questions I wanted to ask you. Thanks for letting me crash your break time. I promise it won't be painful," Peggy said. "My company is trying to find ways to help our people care more about their work. That's why I wanted to talk. As I said earlier, you really seem to care, and based on what you said earlier, others around here do as well. How is that possible?"

"We talk with people."

"Please tell me more."

"We have real conversations. I think that's the magic."

"Conversations with who about what?"

"With customers. We really do want to understand what they want and need. We try to ask the right questions and listen intently to their responses."

"Okay, that makes sense. What else?"

"We have a lot of conversations with our leaders."

"What do you talk about?"

"The vision, our priorities, our performance, our struggles, hopes, and dreams too."

"Seriously?" Peggy, trying not to reveal her amazement, knew her company didn't have those kinds of conversations. "What's the vision for this place?"

"To make the world more beautiful . . . every day."

"That's a powerful idea. Any other conversations I should know about?"

"Well . . . we talk to each other a lot too."

"Who are you referring to?"

"My fellow employees. You might even say we do life together. We talk about triumphs and tragedies, fears, failures, and struggles. We talk about how to help each other."

We talk about triumphs and tragedies, fears, failures, and struggles.

"We've been exploring the power of connection to drive engagement. I know you didn't use the word, but it sounds like you are really connected to your customers, your coworkers, and your organization," Peggy said, testing what she had just heard. "And you believe conversations are the primary driver?"

"I can't comprehend any other way to make it happen," Betty said, looking at the clock, "I need to go back to work. Thanks for the coffee. Do you still want your flowers?"

Environment

Kim and Gary were given the assignment to explore the concept of Environment.

"I'm just not sure," Gary huffed.

"Which part doesn't make sense to you?" Kim asked.

"Environment is such a catchall. You can put anything in this category. It's not a principle—it's a black hole!"

"Hold on. I don't think that was Blake's intent at all. Remember what he said about the Renaissance?"

"Probably not," Gary said.

"He said the elements were perfect that combined to create the Renaissance." She continued, "Do you remember the things he mentioned?"

"No."

Referring back to her notes, Kim read, "There was no single factor that resulted in the Renaissance; it burst into history as a result of talent, collaboration fueled by proximity, resources, and perhaps most importantly, the mindset of the people. All of this created extreme levels of care, even passion. That doesn't sound like a catchall to me."

"I would eliminate the word *talent*," Gary said.

"Why? That seems important to me," Kim said.

"I'm not saying it's unimportant; I realize a bunch of slackers were not going to give birth to the Renaissance. However, the company is already working on how to attract and retain the best people. Let's not cloud our current work with the mandate to have talented people. That's a blinding flash of the obvious."

"If we acknowledge the importance of talent but take it off the table, that just leaves collaboration, resources, and mindset. Is that enough?"

"I'm *still* not sure," Gary said.

"And your suggestion is . . .?" Kim asked impatiently.

"Don't have one. I'm just not sure about those three," Gary said.

"Acknowledged," Kim said. "But let's not forget our assignment. Can we find a modern-day example in which environmental factors appear to have impacted the level of care exhibited by a group of people?"

"I'm drawing a blank," Gary said.

"I've got a crazy idea," Kim added. "Let's go to a ball game this afternoon."

"Have you lost your mind?" Gary asked. "I don't know about you, but I don't want to walk in to the next meeting and say we really didn't do our assignment, but we had fun at the game."

"Trust me on this. Let's leave around 4:30," she said.

That seems kinda early for a game, Gary thought to himself.

"See you out front!" Kim said over her shoulder as she left the office.

~

The two rode just a few miles to a Little League field. As they approached the park, Gary said, "Okay, so I guess your kid is pitching today?"

"No, he may not play much this afternoon. He's not usually a starter," Kim said.

As the game began, Chris ran over and gave his mom a kiss and a hug. "Thanks for coming, Mom!" he said as he ran back to the dugout.

"How old is Chris?" Gary asked.

"Ten," Kim said.

"Does he love the game?"

"He does now."

"What does that mean?" Gary asked.

"Let me tell you a story," Kim began.

"Last year, this team was a mess. They lost every game—and many of the games were decided by the 'mercy rule.'"

"What's that?"

"When you are ten runs behind and it's the fifth inning, the umpires call the game."

"Sounds painful."

"It's merciful," she smiled. "So, to answer your last question, Chris did *not* love the game last year, but he does now."

"What changed?"

"The environment," Kim smiled.

"Okay, I'll bite. What does that mean for a Little League team?"

"Where to begin? First, they found a sponsor—a local business that would help financially."

"What does that mean?"

"They received new uniforms, bats, and balls, and the catcher got some equipment that fit. Last year, his chest protector hung down below his knees," she said.

"Next, Sam joined the team."

"Is he good?"

"Not really, but his dad owns a landscaping company. They put new grass on the field—well, not new grass, just grass—last season the entire field was dirt."

"I thought the field looked really nice," Gary said.

"Just like the big leaguers," Kim smiled.

"Anything else? Did they change coaches?"

"Yes and no."

"Huh?" Gary uttered.

"The same two dads are coaching, but they changed their approach."

"How?"

"Last year, the coaches never asked the kids if they had any questions. And my guess is, even if they had, no one would have spoken. This year, at least once in every practice, the coaches ask for questions. It has been transformative. I think the children were all too scared to speak last year. This year, I think the coaches have created a safe place for input, questions, and dialogue."

"And their record?" Gary asked.

"They are undefeated: 8 and 0."

"Yeah, but surely to go from worst to first they have added some new players," Gary said skeptically.

"No, just Sam."

"Incredible," Gary said. "So, their outcomes are significantly improved without an influx of new talent."

"More than that, they want to be here. Their engagement—their level of care—has skyrocketed," Kim said. "I know they are just kids, but I think it is a vivid example of setting the right environment for care to take root and people to flourish."

"You convinced me," Gary said. "Look, Chris is on deck!"

Affirmation

Charles was eager to join the search for examples of extraordinary engagement. He began to consider all the places he felt demonstrated high levels of care in their daily activities. Tragically, his list was short. This reality underscored the virtually universal problem organizations are facing with engagement.

Looking for a place for lunch, he decided to eat at a restaurant he had never visited before.

"Good afternoon," a cheerful employee greeted him as soon as he walked in the door. "Will you be dining in or taking out today?"

"Dining in," Charles said.

Before Charles knew what was happening, he found himself immersed in an outstanding dining experience. The food was delivered to his table hot and fresh; someone offered him fresh ground pepper for his salad; another team member came by to "refresh" his beverage; and to top it all off, one of the managers stopped by his table.

"I'm Greg, one of the managers here; I just wanted to check on you and be sure we met your expectations today," he said warmly.

"Thanks for checking on me," Charles said. "This place is bizarre."

"What do you mean, *bizarre*?" A concerned look crept across Greg's face.

"No, no, it's all good." Charles quickly added. "However, the level of care is not normal," he said without thinking. Then it hit him—he might have found his case study.

"If you eat here often, I hope you'll find it to be *normal* for us," the manager said with a smile. "That's the goal. We want every guest to feel cared for personally on every visit."

"It appears to be working," Charles said. "How do you do it?"

"That's a big question," Greg said. "We actually do a lot of things behind the scenes so you can have a consistently amazing experience."

"Can you share with me some of the things you do?" Charles asked.

"It starts with leadership—no organization drifts to greatness."

"Sure, that makes sense," Charles agreed. "What else?"

"We have to select the right people and be sure they are aligned on what matters most—this is a never-ending challenge, but without it, everything is *so* much harder; some things even become impossible without everyone pulling in the same direction."

"Got it. Anything else?"

It starts with leadership—no organization drifts to greatness.

"Probably two more big ideas," Greg continued. "We have to be sure the people are fully engaged and focused on execution. If they aren't engaged, there's no way we'll deliver consistently. We want excellence to be the norm, not a random occurrence."

"Very impressive," Charles said. "Thanks for sharing! Do you have time for one follow-up question?"

"Sure."

"Let's go back to the idea of 'fully engaged'; my organization has been thinking about that a lot."

"What have you decided?" Greg asked.

"It's *really* hard!" Charles laughed.

"We agree. That's why we work on it every day."

"What do you *actually do* to foster high levels of engagement?"

"You ask *really* hard questions," Greg laughed. "We do several things."

"Give me just one example." Charles didn't want to beg, but he would if he had to.

"Okay, just two words: *thank you*!"

"I'm not sure I follow you," Charles admitted.

"We want every employee to know how much we value their energy and effort, so we say thank you a lot," Greg said.

Charles knew he had a puzzled look on his face. "Please say more about that."

"We say thank you when we see an employee doing their work with excellence; we say thank you when we observe someone going above and beyond our already high standards; we say thank you when we see our people living out our core values; we even say thank you for a team member's contributions at the end of every shift."

"Hold on. I was with you until that last example," Charles said. "Practically, how do you do that?"

"If I am here, I thank every team member when his or her shift is over. If I am not here—I do have a life outside of work," he smiled, "one of the other managers steps in and thanks people for their work. It has become part of our culture."

"Doesn't it get old?" Charles asked.

"I guess if it were not genuine, but when it is from the heart, it tends to connect with the heart. But don't miss the bigger idea here: people who are appreciated will be much more engaged than those whose efforts are not acknowledged."

"And you seriously think high levels of affirmation make a difference?" Charles asked.

"How was your experience today?"

"Sorry, bad question," Charles said. "Something is obviously working. Greg, let me say thank you for sharing your time and your insights. And, thanks for a remarkable experience."

"We hope to see you again soon," Greg said.

"You will!"

Responsibility

Rose and Ben were scheduled to attend a one-day workshop the next day. They discussed not attending given the impending deadline but decided the day out of the office might give them a fresh perspective. Besides, the session they were scheduled to attend just *might* have some bearing on their assignment. The morning of the workshop, they met early for a quick breakfast.

"I hope attending this workshop is a good decision," Rose said.

"I think we'll be fine. Did you read the course description?" Ben asked.

"Yeah, but I don't remember the details," Rose admitted. "All I know is this guy is supposed to be one of the best at designing training events."

"The description sounds good to me." Ben proceeded to read from his phone: "Learn how to increase learning, retention, and engagement."

"Intriguing," Rose said. "Let's take good notes."

"We're going to do better than that," Ben added.

"What have you got in mind?"

"We're going to take our instructor to dinner tonight."

"We are?" Rose said in disbelief.

"Yes, we are," Ben said.

"How did you arrange that?"

"Haven't done it yet, but I will as soon as we can get into the room."

When the two found their seats, it was still thirty minutes until the program was scheduled to begin. Ben said, "Let's find our dinner guest."

Approaching the technicians at the back of the room, Ben introduced himself and found out the speaker had not yet checked in for his microphone.

"We'll wait here," Ben said to Rose. "He'll be here soon." No sooner had Ben finished his sentence than Jerry Bushman approached the table.

"Good morning, Mr. Bushman! My name is Ben, and this is my colleague, Rose. We're excited about your workshop."

"Thanks for your enthusiasm, and you can call me Jerry," he said.

"Thanks, Jerry. I know you have to get ready to speak, but I was wondering if we could buy you dinner tonight."

"Really? Why would you want to do that?" Jerry asked.

"Honestly, we're working on a project I think you would be interested in."

"But we're not selling anything," Rose quickly added.

"Right, we're not selling anything, but we are searching the globe to determine what causes people to really care about their work. We'd love to share what we've learned thus far and get any counsel you might have for us," Ben said.

"It would need to be an early dinner," Jerry said.

"You name the time and the place," Ben said.

"Let's meet in front of the stage at the end of the day," Jerry said.

"Outstanding," Rose said. "We'll see you then."

The workshop was surprisingly applicable to the topic of engagement. Jerry provided many ideas regarding how to help learners care more about whatever content one was trying to impart. Ben and Rose both learned a lot and were excited to continue the conversation with Jerry over dinner.

~

"Thanks for agreeing to have dinner with us!" Rose said.

"Thanks for the invitation," Jerry said. "When you travel as much as I do, eating alone gets old. Besides, I am interested in what you're learning about how to help people really care. I've been trying to do the same thing for decades."

"Yes, we could tell," Ben said. "We heard a lot today we believe will be helpful in our efforts."

"Please tell me more about your work," Jerry requested.

Rose and Ben began to talk about some of what Blake and Megan had discovered during their travels.

"Fascinating!" Jerry said. "I really do think you guys are onto something. How can I help?"

"We're at the stage in our process where we are trying to figure out how to apply some of the ideas . . . translate the principles into practice," Ben said.

"Ben and I have been asked to find real-world examples of how to engender higher levels of Responsibility."

"Why didn't you say that earlier?" Jerry chuckled. "I hope you saw dozens of examples in the workshop today."

"I think we did, but could you summarize your point of view for us?" Ben asked.

"Sure, as I stressed throughout the day, one of the problems with the way people approach training is that way too much of the responsibility falls to the instructor. The best way to get learners to engage, or care, is to shift the responsibility to the student. This is the magic behind my method. If I go back to my hotel in the evening and I'm tired, I didn't do it right. The students should be tired, not me!

"Let's go back through your notes from today and see how I practiced this principle," Jerry said.

After a quick review, Ben and Rose realized the entire day was focused on shifting the responsibility to the learner—not just ownership of the outcomes, but the methods, too, were often created by the learners.

"No wonder I'm so tired," Rose laughed.

"My work here is complete," Jerry said with a big smile.

"Any final advice for us?" Ben asked.

"I can't really speak to all the drivers of engagement, or caring, as you describe it, but I have spent decades teaching one big idea around the globe: if you can shift enough responsibility to your students, or employees, so they feel ownership for the work, your outcomes will improve. I think that's what Blake and Megan have also discovered."

If you can shift enough responsibility to your students, or employees, so they feel ownership for the work, your outcomes will improve.

"Is it shifting or sharing?" Rose asked.

"Fair question," Jerry said. "*Sharing* is probably the better word choice. However, the people I work with usually have such a death grip on responsibility, I have to overstate the transfer to get their attention. What you are suggesting is more accurate. Leaders do not generally shift responsibility as much as they share it . . . the leader is still ultimately accountable."

"Thanks for the clarification. What you are suggesting appears to be a powerful way to improve engagement," Ben said. "One final question . . ."

"Sure."

"How do you know this idea of sharing responsibility really works?" Ben asked.

"The test."

"What test?" Rose asked.

"There should always be a test," Jerry said with a faint smile. "When you shift responsibility, you must always go back to see if you were successful. The test may be very literal if you are a classroom teacher. Or in the marketplace, I guess the accountability naturally accompanies any task or assignment. If you got it right, the employees will too . . . you have to verify the results to be sure. Were the desired behaviors observed? Were the desired outcomes achieved? These are the ultimate 'test' questions."

Huddle

"Good morning! I trust you all had fun with your action item." Charles smiled.

Rose spoke up first: "I have to confess, I was not sure about any of this. I left our last meeting thinking we had just joined Blake on his wild goose chase . . . *without* the chance to travel the world! Now, I feel like he and Megan may be onto something."

"I'm glad you feel better," Charles said. "Why don't you and Ben go first; what did you find?"

"We were trying to find an example in which responsibility played a significant role in a person's level of engagement and caring. We found it!"

"Where to begin?" Ben said, thinking back on their experience.

"I've got this," Rose said. She told the group about the workshop and their dinner with Jerry Bushman. "He told us his entire philosophy and career has been built on the premise that if you can share responsibility for learning with the learner, their level of care, concern, and attention will go to a whole new level. We believe the same will happen with employees."

"How do you do that—'share' responsibility?" Gary asked.

"He has many techniques, but the big idea is simple: leaders must be willing to actually give people responsibility! Create a culture in which sharing responsibility is the norm, not the exception. Give people real responsibility for goals, methods, and decisions, whenever it makes sense."

"Thanks. Who's next? Gary, can you and Kim tell us what you found?" Charles asked.

They gave a quick report on the dramatic turnaround on Chris's team—apparently due to the changes in the environment since last season.

"It has been unbelievable," Kim concluded. "Last year, Chris said he didn't think he ever wanted to play baseball again—he said he didn't *care* about the team. Now, he eats and sleeps baseball. Before we started this work, I couldn't begin to describe the change. But now, looking back, I think it was almost exclusively about the environment. The 'how' is simply to look at what people really need to win, pun intended, both physically and emotionally, and provide it. The environment was the barrier—the kids had the talent all along."

"Okay, thanks!" Charles said. "Peggy?"

"I was trying to think about where I had personally experienced what felt like high levels of care.

Then, I was buying some flowers when I met Betty. She was phenomenal! So, I asked her if we could chat over a cup of coffee, and we did. She really simplified their approach to connection—she said they talk to people! Customers, leaders, and coworkers. Real conversations are the bridge to real connections," Peggy said.

Real conversations are the bridge to real connections.

"I'm glad you enjoyed your coffee with Betty," Rose said, "but I've been thinking about Connection, and I'm not so sure."

"What's your hesitation?" Ben asked.

"It's obvious civil rights was, and still is, a cause for the ages, but when we think of our organization—no disrespect intended, Charles—we're not a cause."

"Good point. What we do is clearly not an ethical or moral cause, but do any of you think the idea of Connection can still apply?" Charles asked.

"I'm not sure. For a lot of people, this is just a job." Gary voiced what others were thinking.

"Do you think if people were connected to the vision, that would help?" Charles asked.

"I think it might," Rose said, "if the vision is something people can actually connect with."

"Say more about that," Peggy said.

"Well, if the vision is *just* about shareholder value, I'm not sure how much people are going to care, but if it has a higher, more noble purpose, something to do with adding value to others, maybe," Rose concluded.

"Very interesting," Peggy said. "Betty told me she really felt connected to the vision of her organization—they want to make the world more beautiful every day."

"Sounds like connection to a cause to me," Ben added.

"One more thing," Peggy added. "I think Connection is bigger than Blake painted it. Sure, connection to others and the vision matters, but Betty was also connected to her customers. She cared enough to ask thoughtful questions and listen. And, when time allowed, she wanted to know the story behind their purchase. All of this was made possible by the conversations."

"Thanks, Peggy. I guess it's my turn," Charles said.

"Like Peggy, I sort of fell into my case study. I went to a restaurant I had not visited previously and was blown away."

"By what?" Kim asked.

"All of it . . . the people, the food, the level of hospitality, the involvement of leadership—one of the managers came to check on me."

"I've seen that before, but I never felt like they really care. It's almost like it's on a checklist or something," Gary said.

"Exactly," Charles said. "Rarely do I feel cared for at a quick service restaurant, but this place was different."

"Okay, we're ready. What's the punchline? Did you learn anything about Affirmation?" Rose asked.

"I did. Greg, the manager I mentioned earlier, was very generous with his time and information about the culture he and the other leaders are trying to create. Honestly, it sounded a lot like the ideas Blake has been discussing with us for years. However, I didn't get into all of that with Greg. I asked him how they were able to create such high levels of engagement by their employees—it felt like they really care. He started by saying it was complicated, and they, in fact, do many things; however, I didn't let him off the hook."

"What did he say?" Rose asked, growing impatient with all the buildup.

"He said their secret sauce was *thank you*."

"What does that mean?" Ben asked.

"Loosely translated, they are creating a culture of affirmation when they express genuine appreciation to their employees. They affirm people multiple times every day."

"And the result?" Kim asked.

"I had a fabulous experience. I want us all to go there for lunch so you can see for yourself. No question, they have harnessed the power of affirmation!"

BOB

Megan and Blake decided to make what they believed to be their last field trip a short one. They had only one place to visit and, as far as they knew, no one to really talk to—there were no guides for the small town in west Texas. After their flight landed, they rented a car and headed west. After about an hour, they were still in the suburbs and quickly approaching their destination.

"This is strange," Megan said. "According to the National Register, the ranch we're looking for should be a couple hundred thousand acres. I wonder why all I can see are houses and gas stations."

"Don't know," Blake said. "According to the GPS, we should be really close."

When they turned the corner, they were looking at the biggest shopping mall they had ever seen.

"This must be a mistake," Megan said. "According to the records, the ranch is . . . here. Let's park and see what we can find out."

As they drove around the mall, trying to decide where to park, Megan said, "Stop, stop the car!"

Startled and frustrated, Blake slammed on the brakes. "What?"

"Over there, look." She pointed across the lot.

"What are you pointing at?" Blake asked. "It looks like a gas station."

"No, behind the station. Drive over there."

As they approached, Blake saw what she was talking about: a large weathered bronze plaque.

Blake said, "You have eagle eyes!"

Standing in the afternoon sun, Megan read the inscription aloud:

> **NHH RANCH**
> **1794–2005**
>
> ---
>
> The most influential ranch in Texas history. Covering a land mass of over 200,000 acres, employing over 10,000 women and men, raising over 1.5 million head of cattle, and feeding our troops during two world wars, all while pioneering a new leadership paradigm built on genuine care for people.

When she finished, there was an awkward silence. "Should we go home? Should we cry?"

Blake finally said, "We were so close."

"Did you notice the second date? It's 2005 . . . just after your dad died," Megan said.

"I wonder if Dad ever met Bob?"

"Remember, Robert, on the registry, was the original owner," Megan said.

"Oh yeah. I wonder who Bob was on Dad's note?"

"I'm not sure; I'm just trying to put the pieces together," she said.

"Me too. Here's the story I've just made up—Dad did all the work we've been reenacting; it took him years. Then, late in his journey, he discovered this place. Based on the reference to a 'leadership paradigm built on genuine care for people,' Bob or whoever was probably doing the things we discovered."

"Yes, the reference to care is interesting. We've said engagement is about genuine care. I wonder how that might connect," Megan said. "And what does NHH stand for anyway?"

Blake turned to go but stopped and gave Megan that look—the one of determination she had seen so many times before.

"Hold on. Someone sold this ranch to the developer. I'm assuming, or hoping, it was a descendent of Robert. Who knows? Maybe it was Bob himself. Let's run that down!" Blake said.

"Let's start at the mall office," Megan agreed.

The couple made their way past scores of shops and kiosks to a back corridor and found the mall office. After they explained their situation, the receptionist finally gave in and let them speak to Jill Matthews, the mall manager.

"This is a highly unusual request, but I'm sure Bob won't mind," Jill said.

"Bob?" Megan said. "There is a Bob?"

"Yes, he is the gentleman whose family sold us this property."

"My Dad had a note with Bob's name on it!" Blake said.

"Here's his address—it's not far from here. If you see him, please tell him I said hi."

~

On the way to Bob's house, Megan said, "Do you have questions for Bob? We never really talked about that."

"I do. And you?"

"I want him to help us connect the Renaissance and Selma and all the other pieces."

"That's a tall order, but we'll see."

The couple drove the short two miles to an upscale community of large homes on very large lots.

"I guess if your previous front yard was two hundred thousand acres, you wouldn't want to live in a townhome," Megan said.

"If you sold two hundred thousand acres, you can live anywhere you want," Blake added.

Blake rang the doorbell, and the couple was greeted by an elderly man, trim and well dressed.

"May I help you?" he said.

"Are you Bob?"

"Yes, I am. And who are you?"

"I'm Blake Brown, and this is my wife, Megan. Jill Matthews, from the mall, gave us your address—she said to tell you hi!"

"That's nice. She's a lovely woman. Is that why you came . . . to deliver her message?"

"No, sir. It's a little bit complicated. We've been traveling the world chasing clues left by my father—he died about fifteen years ago. And the last clue has brought us here."

"Who was your father?"

"Jeff Brown."

"Jeff! I loved Jeff! Come in, come in. So sorry for the 'twenty-questions' routine. I just feel like I need to be careful who I invite into my home."

"Certainly," Megan said.

"You knew my dad?" Blake said.

"I loved your dad—a gifted man and an amazing leader."

"How did you know him?"

"I knew your father because he, not unlike you, knocked on my door many years ago."

"What did he want?"

"He asked me if I would be his mentor."

"Seriously?" Blake said.

"Wow!" Megan said.

"I told him no," Bob said.

"What?"

"I told him I wouldn't be his mentor. Instead, if he wanted, we could be friends and help each other."

"What made you say that?" Megan asked.

"I had heard Jeff speak at a conference a couple of years before he showed up here, so his reputation preceded him; I knew our relationship could be mutually beneficial."

"How long did you know each other?"

"Not long enough," Bob said sadly.

"Thank you for loving my dad," Blake said. "I'm sure he valued his time with you."

"How can I serve you today?" Bob asked.

Win the Heart

Blake and Megan spent the next few minutes setting the context for their big adventure. They explained at a high level Blake's current challenge with the engagement of his organization and how this led him to discover his father's book project.

"Yes," Bob said, "I knew about the book. Your dad's research led him to Texas. We were known in small circles as innovative with our people practices, and he came here to see what he could learn. However, in the end, I learned far more from him."

"Okay, where should we begin?" Megan asked. "We would love to know what you learned from each other."

"Maybe we should start with a little history lesson," Bob said.

"Sounds good," Blake said.

Bob walked to a cabinet and pulled out a large photo album. He handed it to Megan.

"My great-great-great-great-grandfather won the ranch in a poker game, or at least the first parcel of land. That was 1794. He was the first innovator in our family—always looking for ways to make the ranch and the people better. He's the one who named this place and established our brand."

"Tell us about that. What does NHH stand for?"

"There's a picture of the front gate—he put that up around 1800. Can you read it? Photo quality was crappy in those days."

Megan squinted and said, "No Hired Hands."

"NHH," Bob said. "That's our brand, but it has always been more than a brand—it's a deeply held belief system. You see, Pops, as everyone called him, believed in human worth and dignity at least a century before it was cool," Bob smiled.

"He was clearly ahead of his time," Blake said.

"I'll say! I still don't think most leaders in the world get it," Bob added.

"Okay, let's be clear—what is the 'it' you are referring to?" Megan asked.

"If you just hire a man's hands, you miss the opportunity to win his heart!" Bob's energy ticked up a notch. "Pops knew this intuitively. He spent his life trying to care for his people. He believed if he demonstrated genuine care for his people, in return, the people would care deeply about their work. He passed that philosophy down to his son, who passed it to his, and so on. It's the only way I knew to lead, so it became my approach as well.

"Let me show you something." Bob got up, walked to a nearby wall, and removed a shadow box that was about twelve inches square with a dark walnut frame.

"This is what Jeff and I talked about on our last visit just before he died."

The three looked down into the shallow box, which contained a single item on a background of white velvet. It was a heart made of what appeared to be a horseshoe.

If you just hire a man's hands, you miss the opportunity to win his heart!

"Tell us the story," Blake said eagerly.

"Pops received this from Horace, his blacksmith, just before Horace's death. Mildred, Horace's wife, said it was the last thing he ever made. He gave it to Pops and said thank you for all the care he showered on him and his family . . . and everyone else who worked for him.

"This simple, primitive heart became a constant reminder to Pops; he kept it on his desk for the rest of his life to remind him of his opportunity as a leader. Here's what Pops knew: Success is not found in a man's hands; it's the heart that makes all the difference! A real leader wins hearts! This was his daily reminder—you can train hands, but you must win hearts."

"Will you tell us about what you referred to as your 'approach?'" Blake said.

"Truthfully, for generations, it was more of an overarching philosophy built on the idea of demonstrating genuine care for our employees. We were successful, but our methods were very loose, random really. That's what I told your dad on his first visit. Together, we were trying to articulate *how* to truly win the hearts of our people. We knew that if we could figure this out, everyone would benefit."

"That's the fundamental question," Blake said. "How do we win the hearts of our people?"

"This is what your dad had been traveling the world trying to discover. And I think he found it! The clarity he brought to this issue was refreshing. In many ways, he gave language to what my family had been trying to do for over two centuries," Bob said.

"What had he learned? Can you tell us?" Megan's voice strained.

"You tell me what you've been able to piece together," Bob said. "I'll let you know if you're close."

Megan and Blake recounted their travels from Selma to Green Bay and the tentative conclusions from each visit.

Megan concluded the world tour: "We believe Connection, Environment, Affirmation, and Responsibility are the drivers of genuine care."

"What do you think? Did we get it right? Did we miss anything?" Blake asked anxiously.

"Is there anything else?" Bob asked.

"Well . . ." Blake said, "not, unless you can tell us something more. We've exhausted all our clues."

Megan interrupted, "You have affirmed one thing today: the leader's goal should be to win the heart; that is the capstone—the big idea linking all of this together."

"You are correct; I think your father and I agreed on that. Anything else?" he added with a wry smile, as if he were baiting them a little bit.

"No, sir. I'm sorry, that's all we've got," Blake said.

"You are almost there." Bob flashed a huge smile. "It is hard to believe you've been able to recreate your father's work so well. You've only missed one little detail."

"Yes . . .?" Megan said nervously.

"Okay, our philosophy is built on the foundational premise that people who really care do better work. They have more energy and enthusiasm and contribute more . . . their discretionary effort increases significantly."

Bob continued, "The answer, as it turned out, was for us, as leaders, to consciously and proactively provide the critical elements needed for care to flourish: Connection . . ." Bob paused for effect before stating the next element: "Affirmation . . ."

Before he could finish, Blake burst into the conversation: "Responsibility and Environment!"

Megan laughed out loud. "It spells CARE! Could it have been more obvious?"

Blake joined her in laughing at themselves. "It may be obvious now," Blake said, "but standing on the Edmund Pettus Bridge, it wasn't clear at all."

"Now, you have the whole story. The key to higher levels of care by employees is for leaders to provide the cornerstones of CARE," Bob said.

"CARE produces caring," Megan offered.

"Bob, you just used a word I've not considered—you called these cornerstones. I've been thinking of them as drivers. Will you say more about your choice of language?" Blake asked.

"Gladly. You can call them anything you want, but for me, *cornerstone* is the best way to describe them. In my day, the cornerstones were the most critical part of any structure—everything rested on them. You'll find, over time, there are countless ways to win the hearts of people, but without the things we've been discussing, your organization will not be as strong as it could be . . . always operating on a shaky foundation.

"Besides, you *drive* cattle," Bob smiled. "You *build* a culture of care."

"Thank you!" Blake said. "Thanks for opening your home to us, for continuing the legacy of your forefathers, and for being a living example of the principles and practices my dad was trying to learn."

As the couple stood at the door exchanging hugs, it was Megan's turn to be emotional. She knew Bob had influenced Jeff, who in turn had helped Blake become the man he was. Her heart was filled with gratitude for the chance to meet Bob. With tears in her eyes, all she could get out was "Thank you."

"I have a parting question for you, Bob," Blake said.

"Shoot."

"Why did you sell the ranch after all those years?" Blake asked.

"Well, I finally got too old to be a rancher—you know, I'll be ninety-five years young this year."

"Congratulations!" Megan said.

"Thanks—I've been blessed in so many ways." Bob paused. "Back to your question . . . We had a family meeting and discussed the fact that my son, who is now seventy-five, didn't want to be in the business anymore—he wanted to go fishing! Can you imagine?" He chuckled. "So, we decided we could do a lot of good with the cash. We started a foundation to help folks in developing countries learn how to build their own successful ranches. We liked the idea of passing on what we've learned," Bob said.

"Sounds like a wonderful cause," Blake said.

"Now, I have one final question for you," Bob said.

"Yes, sir?"

"Are you going to finish your dad's book?"

"I had not really planned to," Blake said.

"I think you should," Bob said.

"I'll consider it . . . only if you agree to write the foreword."

"Deal," Bob said.

The Future

After Blake and Megan returned home and checked on the kids, they went immediately to the basement. Megan was eager to update the big board again.

"It makes so much sense now," she said.

"Agreed," Blake said.

"All the articles, notes, photos, and other artifacts fit," Megan said. "What's next?"

"I want to meet with Charles and the team right away. I want to share with them what we learned in Texas."

"Should I take the board down?" Megan asked.

"No, leave it up for now."

"Are you thinking about Bob's challenge?"

"Yes, I am. 'Write a book' has never been on my list of life goals, but . . ." Blake stopped.

"I know—for your dad," she said.

"Maybe. I'm not ready to commit today; let's put some of what we've learned into practice first. If we see the gains I expect, we'll revisit the book idea."

The next morning, Blake asked Charles and the team for a short meeting.

Blake opened the conversation: "Thanks for coming to yet another unplanned meeting; I truly appreciate your flexibility. Today, I want to give you my final update on our quest to learn the keys to creating a fully engaged workforce."

"How do you know you're finished?" Kim asked.

"Well," Blake began, "The more I've thought about what creates a place where people genuinely care about their work, their coworkers, and their organization, the more I believe there are many contributing factors, but our trip to Texas pulled it all together for me."

Blake proceeded to tell the team about his visit with Bob. "His parting challenge to me was this: You cannot build an enduring great organization with hired hands. You must win hearts.

"So even though I'm not convinced we've discovered *all* the factors affecting someone's level of care, the cornerstones we've identified seem to be enough. I think we're done."

"Win the heart . . . Haven't we heard that language before?" Charles asked.

"Yes, yes, we have. It is the same language Jack used when he was coaching me years ago. He had it right all along. Now, we've just learned a few more best practices to make it real in our organization," Blake said.

"This is incredible!" Peggy said. "It's like a script for a movie."

"It is unbelievable, but there's one more piece—the final piece of the puzzle for me." Blake stepped to the board and said, "Let's review the four cornerstones we identified previously. What were they?"

"Connection," Peggy said.

"Environment," Charles added.

"Affirmation," Kim said.

"And Responsibility," Rose said.

"Exactly," Blake said. He then wrote the four words on the board in the "correct" order:

Connection

Affirmation

Responsibility

Environment

The response from the team caught Blake by surprise. They began to clap—slowly at first—and then they stood.

"Thank you, thank you . . . you can sit down now," Blake said.

"That is amazing!" Peggy said.

"It is cool," Blake agreed.

"So, if the objective is to win the heart of every employee, the strategy is for leaders to provide the cornerstones of CARE," Charles summarized.

"It's elegant in its simplicity: CARE builds the foundation for caring," Kim said.

"And if people care more, everyone wins . . . the employee, their coworkers, our customers, vendors, and the organization overall," Gary said. "I like it."

It's elegant in its simplicity: CARE builds the foundation for caring.

"What's next?" Kim asked.

"We need to let our people know what we've learned and our plan for moving forward," Charles said.

"And," Blake interjected, "we need to start doing the things we've discovered. I'll make that our promise when I address the staff."

"I love it," Rose said. "Please tell them the whole story . . . the clues, the travel, etcetera."

"I can do that. Let's schedule another meeting for the entire staff," Blake said. "Let me know when you want to do it, and I'll be ready."

~

For the second time in less than two months, the entire organization was gathered to hear from Blake. Anticipation and honest skepticism filled the air.

"Thanks for coming together this morning. After we announced this meeting, several of you thanked me. You said you never thought we would follow through on our promise to follow up with you. For that, I am sorry. I am sorry that we have not yet earned your trust. I understand why . . . as human beings, we give our trust to those we deem to be trustworthy. That is one of the problems we are going to solve. Today is the next step on the journey.

"I asked you to complete a survey to help us better assess the state of the business from your perspective. You did, over 80 percent of you. Thank you! Who knows? If we demonstrate ourselves trustworthy, that number may be even higher in the future.

"So, what did we learn? There is much work to be done. Stated in terms of engagement, ours is low. For this, I apologize as well. When engagement is low in an organization, it is *not* the fault of the employees. Leadership is responsible—we must create a workplace that generates massive levels of care. We have not done that.

Leadership is responsible—we must create a workplace that generates massive levels of care.

"Where to next? What do we do with this information? I'm glad you asked!" Blake smiled.

"Collecting this type of data is easy; acting on it is far more challenging. I recently learned my father, a man who led an organization very similar to ours, faced this same challenge almost twenty years ago.

"He traveled the world visiting places and meeting people who might shed light on the challenge of creating a culture of full engagement. Megan and I have been retracing his steps. We've unearthed some insights we believe will be helpful. It all came together when we met Bob, a rancher in Texas.

"He shared his experience as a seventh-generation business owner. We were challenged by his premise: No Hired Hands. Rather, he insisted, we should work to create a workplace that will generate massive levels of genuine care . . . We have to win the heart!

"That's our goal here from this day forward. We need your heart as much as your hands. We are going to focus on four areas we believe will make it much easier for you to care. Bob called them the cornerstones of CARE: Connection, Affirmation, Responsibility, and Environment. When we get these right, you will be free to do your best work every day.

"This is our near-term plan. We will continue to listen and learn together. We can and will make this a great place to work.

"One of my goals is for you to reach the end of your career and say, 'I worked in an organization where we all cared deeply about our work, our coworkers, and our organization . . . and it made all the difference in the world!'"

Epilogue

The weeks ahead were challenging. Bad habits die hard, but Blake and his team were dedicated to rekindling the spirit of care within their organization—their own renaissance of sorts.

Everyone realized skepticism was high and trust was low. The leaders agreed the first step would be to work on Connection. They began immediately to schedule time with their team members to talk. For some, this was challenging, but Charles's team created a few conversation starters to help. The initial goal: open the lines of communication—not with emails and videos but face-to-face.

Affirmation was harder; the leaders thought they were doing a lot of it, but the team disagreed. Creating a culture in which affirmation was the norm would prove to be real work and wouldn't happen quickly. Leaders began to ask their team members to tell them about their favorite recognition. Their answers made Affirmation easier, more personal, and more effective.

Responsibility proved to be the most difficult of the cornerstones to embrace. The current leaders largely believed their job was to own everything—including decisions. Charles and his team updated the annual leadership talent review to include an evaluation of each leader's demonstrated ability to share real responsibility, including decisions. Any leader who wanted a promising future with the company would have to learn to empower others.

The Environment began to change immediately. Blake's remarks to the staff were the catalyst. The comments from the original assessment also gave the leaders a "hit list" of factors impeding the creation of a caring and vibrant workplace. They began to attack them one by one. Each positive action fueled the next: as Connection, Affirmation, and Responsibility improved, so did the overall Environment. As Blake walked the halls of the office or the factory floor, he could once again feel the energy of the culture.

Charles and his team decided to create their own engagement survey based on the cornerstones of CARE. They also decided to conduct quarterly focus groups with employees to monitor the culture change and solicit ideas to accelerate the journey. These meetings kept the issues top of mind for everyone and prevented the busyness of the business from suffocating their good intentions.

The global scavenger hunt rekindled Megan's passion for the world of work beyond the four walls of her home. She decided to reenter the workforce; law school was back on her list of personal goals—after she helped Blake with his next big project.

Blake agreed to finish his father's book after the company had successfully created the culture he and his leaders were advocating and the data had proved it. They would have to become a living example of the transformational power of CARE. Then, and only then, would he be ready to fulfill his father's dream and tell the world how to win the heart of an entire organization. Everyone knew the book would be written sooner rather than later!

Acknowledgments

For me, writing is a team sport. And just as with a successful sports team, only a few players may be on the field at any point in time, but in reality, many others have contributed to the game and the same is true for the book you now hold in your hand.

As I think of the women and men who have influenced the content in this book, the list is very, very long. My memory strains under the assignment to call all of their names to mind. Honestly, I believe I could list a thousand people who have helped me understand the power of full engagement.

Obviously, this is not the place for that list, but I want to acknowledge three distinct groups.

Thanks to all the people I have had the privilege to lead over the last forty years. I have learned so much from you! You have made me and our organization better. Thanks for your patience with me as I tried, and sometimes failed, to create a place where you could really care.

I have also benefited by hanging around some amazing leaders and role models for four decades. I am an eyewitness to the power of the cornerstones of CARE—they work! The Chick-fil-A Operators are another source of learning and inspiration. If you can build a multimillion-dollar business and execute with excellence all while employing a largely teenage workforce, you obviously know a lot about engagement. Thanks to all of you!

I could not conclude this section without thanking some of the people who helped turn my early ideas into a finished product. First, my wife, Donna, reads everything I write—and makes all of it better, starting with punctuation! Steve Piersanti, from Berrett-Koehler, is my chief editor. Although I always try his patience, he has a gift for pushing me to clarity. Thank you, Steve! Randy Gravitt is the final member of the core editorial team. As a seasoned leader, friend, and truth-teller, he added tremendous value. Thank you, Randy! Janice Rutledge, Mike McNair, Sara Jane Hope, and Ken Fracaro rounded out the review team—thank you all! Finally, thanks to Jessica Hampton for managing the details of my life so well. Without your diligence and tenacity, this book would not exist.

As I said, I wish time, space, and memory would allow me to thank the hundreds of influencers who have made me a better leader and writer. I am attempting to live the life of a steward; I am working to pass on what you have entrusted to me. I hope you are pleased with this latest effort.

About the Author

Mark Miller is a business leader, bestselling author, and storyteller.

Mark started his Chick-fil-A career working as an hourly team member in 1977. In 1978, he joined the corporate staff working in the warehouse and mailroom. Since that time, he has provided leadership for Corporate Communications, Field Operations, Quality and Customer Satisfaction, Training and Development, Leadership Development, and more. During his tenure with Chick-fil-A, the company has grown from seventy-five restaurants to over twenty-four hundred locations with annual sales exceeding $10 billion.

He began writing almost twenty years ago when he teamed up with Ken Blanchard, coauthor of *The One Minute Manager*, to write *The Secret: What Great Leaders Know and Do*. The book you now hold in your hand is his eighth, and he has written seven field guides. With over one million books in print, in more than twenty-five languages, Mark's global impact continues to grow.

In addition to his writing, Mark enjoys speaking to leaders. Over the years, he's traveled to dozens of countries teaching for numerous international organizations. His goal is unchanging: to encourage and equip leaders to change their world.

Mark lives an active lifestyle. As a photographer, he has traveled to some of the world's hardest-to-reach places. Past adventures showcase the majesty of the silverback gorillas in the jungles of Rwanda, the breathtaking beauty of Antarctica, and ancient Nepalese traditions at the base camp of Mount Everest.

Mark has been married to Donna, his high school sweetheart, for over thirty-five years. They have two sons, Justin and David, a daughter-in-law, Lindsay, and two amazing grandchildren, Addie and Logan.

Mark would love to connect with you:

Website: LeadEveryDay.com
Instagram: TMarkMiller
Twitter: @LeadersServe
Cell: 678-612-8441

Go Deeper

Win the Heart Field Guide

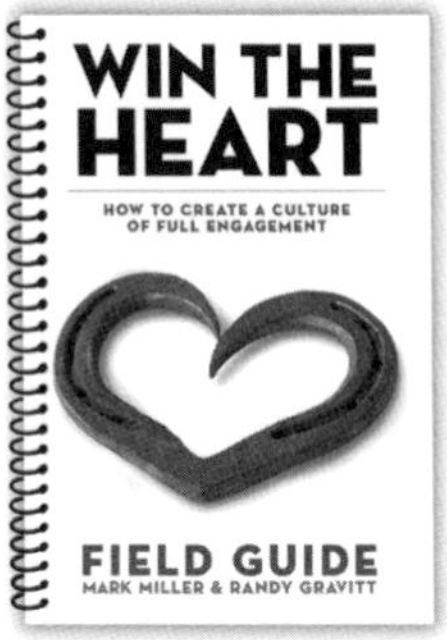

If you want more tactical ideas on how to activate the cornerstones of CARE, this resource is for you. In it you'll find

- Case studies from other organizations
- Sample meeting agendas for your team
- Scores of specific ideas for immediate action
- An assessment you can use to objectively evaluate your current situation and track your progress

Win the Heart Quick Start Guide

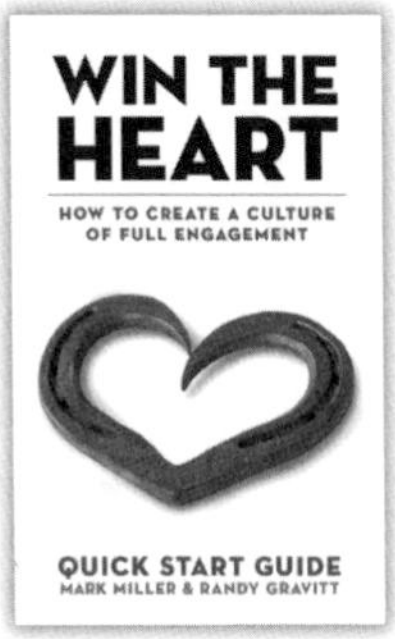

This pocket-sized guide is a great tool for frontline leaders. In it you'll find an overview of the four cornerstones of CARE and specific action items to facilitate their application. Imagine your key leaders working through this resource together. You could literally transform your organization in a matter of months.

Bulk discounts on both these resources are available at LeadEveryDay.com.

Also Part of the High Performance Series

Talent Magnet

How to Attract and Keep the Best People

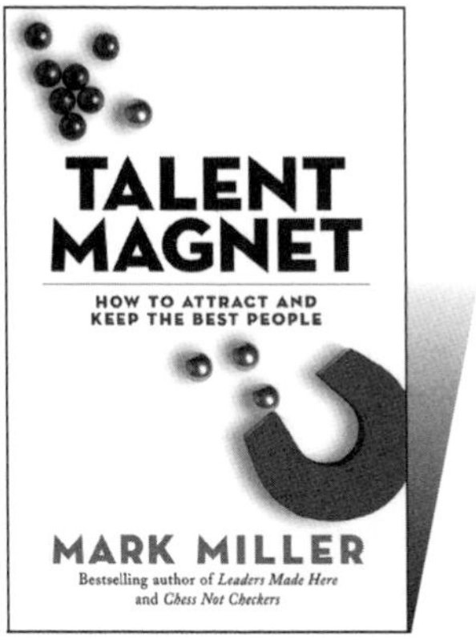

In *Talent Magnet*, Blake Brown, a CEO, is struggling to win the war for talent. At the same time, his sixteen-year-old son, Clint, is looking for his first job. These parallel stories surface insights from both the organization's perspective and the fresh eyes of top talent. These ideas are not born of Miller's imagination. The concepts you will find in *Talent Magnet* are based on extensive research with thousands of participants across industries and demographics. The best part: the findings are not abstract and academic—on the contrary, the prescription to create your own *Talent Magnet* is clear and actionable. You can attract and retain more top talent!

Hardcover, 144 pages, ISBN 978-1-5230-9495-0
PDF ebook, ISBN 978-1-5230-9496-7
ePub ebook, ISBN 978-1-5230-9497-4
Digital audio, ISBN 978-1-5230-9499-8

BK Berrett–Koehler Publishers, Inc.
www.bkconnection.com
800.929.2929

Also Part of the High Performance Series

Leaders Made Here

Building a Leadership Culture

Great leaders create great organizations. However, a scarcity of leaders today means a shortfall in performance tomorrow. Don't gamble with your company's future!

Mark Miller describes how to nurture leaders throughout the organization, from the front lines to the executive ranks. *Leaders Made Here* outlines a clear and replicable approach to creating the leadership bench every organization needs.

Hardcover, 144 pages, ISBN 978-1-62656-981-2
PDF ebook, ISBN 978-1-62656-982-9
ePub ebook, ISBN 978-1-62656-983-6
Digital audio, ISBN 978-1-62656-985-0

Chess Not Checkers

Elevate Your Leadership Game

The early days of an organization are like checkers: a quickly played game with mostly interchangeable pieces. But as the organization expands, the same old moves won't cut it anymore. You have to think strategically, plan ahead, and leverage every employee's specific talents—that's chess. Mark Miller outlines four essential strategies that will transform your leadership and your organization!

Hardcover, 144 pages, ISBN 978-1-62656-394-0
PDF ebook, ISBN 978-1-62656-395-7
ePub ebook, ISBN 978-1-62656-396-4
Digital audio, ISBN 978-1-62656-603-3

BK® Berrett–Koehler Publishers, Inc.
www.bkconnection.com
800.929.2929

Also by Mark Miller

The Heart of Leadership

Becoming a Leader People Want to Follow

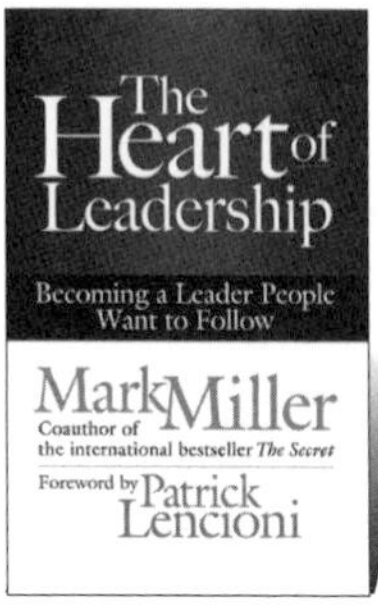

In this enlightening and entertaining business fable, Mark Miller identifies the five unique character traits exhibited by exceptional leaders. When Blake Brown is passed over for a promotion, he is sent on a quest to meet with five of his late father's colleagues, each of whom holds a piece of the leadership puzzle. This book shows us that leadership needn't be the purview of the few—it is within reach for millions around the world.

Hardcover, 144 pages, ISBN 978-1-60994-960-0
PDF ebook, ISBN 978-1-60994-961-7
ePub ebook, ISBN 978-1-60994-962-4

The Secret of Teams

What Great Teams Know and Do

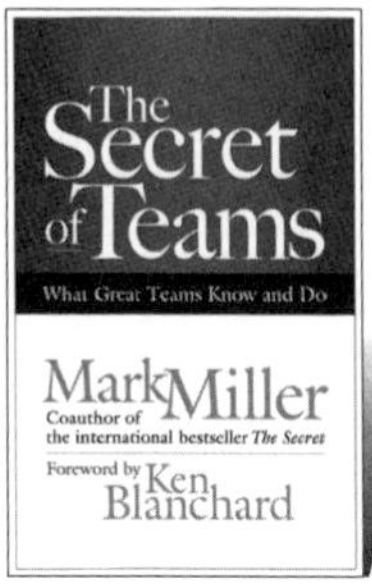

What separates teams that really deliver from the ones that simply spin their wheels? In this book, executive Debbie Brewster learns from three very different teams—the Special Forces, NASCAR, and a local restaurant. Debbie and her team discover the three elements that all high-performing teams have in common, how to change entrenched ways of thinking and acting, how to measure your progress, and more.

Hardcover, 144 pages, ISBN 978-1-60994-093-5
PDF ebook, ISBN 978-1-60994-109-3
ePub ebook, ISBN 978-1-60994-110-9

BK Berrett–Koehler Publishers, Inc.
www.bkconnection.com
800.929.2929

With Ken Blanchard

The Secret

What Great Leaders Know and Do, Third Edition

Join struggling young executive Debbie Brewster as she explores a profound yet seemingly contradictory concept: to lead is to serve. Along the way she learns why great leaders seem preoccupied with the future, what three arenas require continuous improvement, the two essential components to leadership success, how to knowingly strengthen—or unwittingly destroy—leadership credibility, and more.

Hardcover, 144 pages, ISBN 978-1-62656-198-4
PDF ebook, ISBN 978-1-62656-199-1
ePub ebook, ISBN 978-1-62656-200-4

Great Leaders Grow

Becoming a Leader for Life

What is the key ingredient for a long-term, high-impact career in leadership? Debbie Brewster tells Blake Brown, her late mentor's son, "Your capacity to grow determines your capacity to lead" and helps Blake discover and apply four strategies for personal growth. These same strategies can enhance your life and leadership too! Join Blake and explore the path to increased leadership effectiveness and influence.

Hardcover, 144 pages, ISBN 978-1-60994-303-5
PDF ebook, ISBN 978-1-60509-695-7
ePub ebook, ISBN 978-1-60509-696-4

BK
Berrett–Koehler Publishers, Inc.
www.bkconnection.com
800.929.2929

Berrett–Koehler
Publishers

Berrett-Koehler is an independent publisher dedicated to an ambitious mission: *Connecting people and ideas to create a world that works for all.*

Our publications span many formats, including print, digital, audio, and video. We also offer online resources, training, and gatherings. And we will continue expanding our products and services to advance our mission.

We believe that the solutions to the world's problems will come from all of us, working at all levels: in our society, in our organizations, and in our own lives. Our publications and resources offer pathways to creating a more just, equitable, and sustainable society. They help people make their organizations more humane, democratic, diverse, and effective (and we don't think there's any contradiction there). And they guide people in creating positive change in their own lives and aligning their personal practices with their aspirations for a better world.

And we strive to practice what we preach through what we call "The BK Way." At the core of this approach is *stewardship,* a deep sense of responsibility to administer the company for the benefit of all of our stakeholder groups, including authors, customers, employees, investors, service providers, sales partners, and the communities and environment around us. Everything we do is built around stewardship and our other core values of *quality, partnership, inclusion,* and *sustainability.*

This is why Berrett-Koehler is the first book publishing company to be both a B Corporation (a rigorous certification) and a benefit corporation (a for-profit legal status), which together require us to adhere to the highest standards for corporate, social, and environmental performance. And it is why we have instituted many pioneering practices (which you can learn about at www.bkconnection.com), including the Berrett-Koehler Constitution, the Bill of Rights and Responsibilities for BK Authors, and our unique Author Days.

We are grateful to our readers, authors, and other friends who are supporting our mission. We ask you to share with us examples of how BK publications and resources are making a difference in your lives, organizations, and communities at www.bkconnection.com/impact.

Dear reader,

Thank you for picking up this book and welcome to the worldwide BK community! You're joining a special group of people who have come together to create positive change in their lives, organizations, and communities.

What's BK all about?

Our mission is to connect people and ideas to create a world that works for all.

Why? Our communities, organizations, and lives get bogged down by old paradigms of self-interest, exclusion, hierarchy, and privilege. But we believe that can change. That's why we seek the leading experts on these challenges—and share their actionable ideas with you.

A welcome gift

To help you get started, we'd like to offer you a **free copy** of one of our bestselling ebooks:

www.bkconnection.com/welcome

When you claim your **free ebook**, you'll also be subscribed to our blog.

Our freshest insights

Access the best new tools and ideas for leaders at all levels on our blog at ideas.bkconnection.com.

Sincerely,

Your friends at Berrett-Koehler

FSC www.fsc.org MIX Paper from responsible sources FSC® C011935

Certified B Corporation